"Great coaching is priceless. If you want to be a million dollar coach, read this book! In this fascinating work, master coach Alan Weiss puts forth his expansive knowledge and expertise to teach us what it takes to be great in this profession!"

—Marshall Goldsmith, world-renowned executive coach and author of the *New York Times* bestsellers, *MOJO* and *What Got You Here Won't Get You There*

MILLION DOLLAR COACHING

BUILD A WORLD-CLASS PRACTICE BY HELPING OTHERS SUCCEED

ALAN WEISS, PH.D.

New York   Chicago   San Francisco   Lisbon
London   Madrid   Mexico City   Milan
New Delhi   San Juan   Seoul
Singapore   Sydney   Toronto

1 2 3 4 5 6 7 8 9 0   DOC/DOC   1 0 9 8 7 6 5 4 3 2 1 0

ISBN: 978-0-07-174379-2
MHID: 0-07-174379-0

Library of Congress Cataloging-in-Publication Data

Weiss, Alan.
Million dollar coaching : build a world-class practice by helping others succeed / by Alan Weiss.
   p. cm.
  Includes index.
  ISBN 978-0-07-174379-2 (alk. paper)
  1. Personal coaching—Pracice.   2. Counseling—Practice.   I. Tile.
BF637.P36W45   2011
658.3'124—dc22   2010033611

McGraw-Hill books are available at special quantity discounts to use as premiums and sales promotions or for use in corporate training programs. To contact a representative, please e-mail us at bulksales@mcgraw-hill.com.

This book is printed on acid-free paper.

This book is dedicated to my uncle, Irwin Rosenberg, who helped people to laugh. That is a noble calling and a valuable life.

CONTENTS

PREFACE

THE VERY REAL POWER and importance of coaching as a developmental tool is in danger of becoming comfort food, like chicken, or comfort wine, like Merlot. Being coached has become "comfort development."

It's time we stopped that nonsense, and that's what I'm about for the next 300 or so pages.

When I began my organizational development consulting career, my contemporaries and I were constantly coaching executives and managers as part of our assignments. None of us ever dreamed of suggesting that we needed special credentials or separate projects or unique methodologies. We coached and advised people on how best to deal with the changes and improvements that our projects were creating.

How could we not do that? And virtually every person involved in that dynamic gladly accepted the counsel, because we all wanted to maximize our chances for success in the partnership of consultant and client.

On occasion, someone would simply request coaching to improve his or her presentation skills, or ability to close sales, or respond to customer complaints. Fair enough, that was simple, but it was also more effective because we understood organizational realities, such as feedback loops, compensation policies, career development, succession planning, change management, and all the other tools in a good consultant's kit.

If you perform a Google search on coaching as I write this line, you get 61 million entries; if you use "coaching associations," you get 3.6 million; if you use "coaching universities," you get 7 million. You get the idea. Coaching has become an industry rather than a discipline, a cult rather than a corporate norm.

In the pages that follow, I'm going to explain how to provide great coaching and make a million doing it, by focusing on the improvement and results and your value in helping others to help you to help them. This is a great professional pursuit, where doing well by others can provide so much good for you.

These coaching universities and associations can put a dozen initials after your name. That and two dollars will get you on a bus. My intent is to put seven figures into your bank account.

That will get you on easy street.

—Alan Weiss
East Greenwich, RI
January 2011

WHAT ON EARTH IS A COACH?

IF IT'S NOT CLEAR TO YOU, DON'T WORRY; IT'S NOT VERY CLEAR TO ME

WHO CERTIFIES THE CERTIFIERS?

A coach who is very well known today was starting out in the 1990s with no experience, no college education, and, basically, no clue. She asked if she could hang out with me when I visited some clients and prospects, so that she could understand what these engagements were all about.

In a wild fit of goodwill, I said yes.

After some weeks of this, she decided that she was suffi- ciently educated and asked if she could do anything for me in return. I assured her that it was my pleasure, and that nothing was needed. But she persisted.

"There must be something I can coach you about. Tell me something you've always wanted to do but haven't been able to accomplish."

I was getting weary, so I said, "Okay, I've always wanted to host a regular radio show. I've done it once or twice, but I'd love to have a daily program." I figured that if there was any vague possibility that she could help with this, it would be fine with me.

"Right!" she said. "Starting in a couple of days, I'm going to help you with my greatest coaching technique."

Four days later, I received a letter from her. Inside was a card, which said (I am NOT making this up):

"Every day, say three times in the morning, 'I WILL have a radio show, I WILL have a radio show.' Before you know it, your dreams will come true."

I still don't have a radio show, but I have a profound sense of how ridiculous and amateurish the coaching "profession" can be. (Don't forget, this person has been widely seen on television and in print media.)

In a classic five-minute comedy sketch, Bob Newhart portrays a therapist who never takes more than five minutes, and charges a dollar a minute. When a woman reveals that she's afraid of being enclosed in a box and buried, he tells her that there's a two-word cure. She takes out a notebook, and he yells, "STOP IT!!!" When she shares that she also has myriad other issues, he yells, "STOP IT!!!" each time. When she tells him that she's very unhappy with his therapy, he agrees to slow up and says that he'll give her an additional 10-word cure: "STOP IT OR I'LL PUT YOU IN A BOX AND BURY YOU!!!"

What's the "truth" about what constitutes a coach? I can tell you this: it's not attending a program and obtaining a certificate and some arcane initials after your name. No government institution, no academic source, no Gnostic parchments have endowed these programs with the ability to create coaches better than anyone else.

At times, I've had to tell people to "knock it off," a là Newhart, and to stop whining or complaining or opening all baggage. At other times, however, I've had to gingerly explain to a division president that his decline in personal effectiveness and productivity was due to clinical depression (having tested for the indicators), and that he had a disease that needed treatment. These extremes and everything in between are often demanded of a good coach.

So the first thing I want to tell you is that a great many people, although not everyone, can coach. The requisite skills and behaviors are learnable and not natal, but they are not automatically certifiable by having performed certain rituals and made certain tuition payments. Not only have I coached extensively, but I've helped develop coaches all over the world, both within and outside of organizations.

Here are some of the key characteristics that I've assembled:

1. Skills
   - Highly skilled and sensitive listening
   - Superb oral communication, combining both tact and directness
   - A keen ability to observe behavior and detect cognitive dissonance
   - The capability to develop behavioral objectives and metrics for success
   - A combination of "frontstage and backstage" counseling
   - Empathy as distinct from sympathy[1]
   - Minimally, basic consulting skills and organizational knowledge
2. Behaviors
   - High assertiveness, when needed, to overcome procrastination
   - High persuasiveness, to influence and convince

---

[1] Understanding what the other person is feeling without having to feel it yourself, thereby creating an objective response and not a commiseration.

- Moderate patience levels, to listen but not lose momentum
- Moderate detail orientation, to track progress but not overanalyze
- High integrity, to preserve confidentiality
- A high sense of proportion, to place others' behaviors in context
- A healthy ego, convinced that one can help, but not playing the role of "savior"

3. Experiences
- Having been successfully coached oneself
- Organizational experience as an employee
- Interaction with intended client levels as a peer

Note that I haven't included age or amount of experience. Obviously, a younger person may not have had the time to gain some of these requirements, but it's not out of the question. Many mature people who are looking at coaching as a second career still don't have the requisites despite their years at work.

> *Stop it! Don't regard coaching as some kind of dark science or as some lofty cosmic pursuit. It is merely the temporary engagement with a client to help that client improve. The odds are, if you're reading this, you can do it. If you continue reading, you'll probably be able to do it really well.*

Most definitions of coaching include specific disciplines, activities, and regimens. They tend to focus on helping someone become better at certain activities. All of that may be true, but I prefer this:

> *A coach helps someone create a desired result through improved behavior and performance, as mutually determined at the outset.*

Therefore, if you're coaching me, we'll agree from the beginning on how I'll be better when we're done (the output or result) and how we'll know it (the metric or indicators). If we don't establish these things at the outset, then how do we know that we're making progress or are on the right track?

That's why "life coaches" and such designations make zero sense to me. What does that mean? You're going to improve my "life"? I find that most of these coaches aren't coaches at all, but people with predetermined alternatives that they claim have worked for them (did the woman who sent me that card really read something to herself three times a morning?!) and/or for others. Part of the reason that coaching has grown as a pseudo-separate discipline is that it's something of a pet rock: there is a cachet to claiming that you have a personal coach, whether the coach makes sense or not and whether you abide by his or her advice or not.

It's sort of like a piece of art that you put up that you really can't stand or even understand, but you want others to know you can afford it.

I don't think we need some kind of "trend du jour" affectation, nor the conceit that coaching is embedded deep in eschatology. Rather, we need an attitude of professional help. "Professional," because presumably anyone who is reading this book intends to be paid for the value and improvement that he or she provides for clients. And "help" because we are supposed to be improving the client's condition. The Hippocratic Oath's "first, do no harm" is insufficient for our purposes. We shouldn't be paid for leaving the client "as is."

Our mission and our value is in leaving our client better off than when we walked in. That requires a definitive starting point, intermediate steps, and an agreed-upon disengagement. If you're coaching on an indefinite basis, you haven't created an improved condition for your client. You've created codependency.

Some of the earliest references to coaching are actually quite modern. In 1830, the term coach was in use at Oxford to denote instructors, and as you would imagine, by 1831 it was being used in sports. However, "coaching" was going on before the beginning of recorded history, no doubt, as one person showed another how to plant rutabagas, elude a tiger, or deal with an injury.

And while I can't prove it, I'm betting that none of these early, no doubt effective coaches had any initials after their names. Most likely, they didn't even have names.

If you're curious about how good a coach you may already be, see the Appendix for "What's My Coach Quotient (CQ)?"

THE DIFFERENCE BETWEEN A COACH AND A MENTOR

There are various roles that a person can take on when he or she is advising others. For example, one is the therapist, where a Ph.D. or even an MD is earned, certain state requirements must be met, and help ranges from exploration of upbringing and environment to sexual identity, and from periodic 50-minute "hours" to the prescription of medication (and, at times, even incarceration). At the other extreme are "talk radio" call-in shows, where listeners are "diagnosed" and provided with remedial action by someone with few credentials other than the ability to draw high ratings. (One such "doctor" actually had a

Ph.D. in physiology or some such thing, sort of like a famed TV "meteorologist" whose degree was in optometry).

I'm going to leave out the extremes, because otherwise I'd be dealing with graphology, invalid personality tests, fortune cookies, horoscopes, tea leaves, palmists, and psychics. (Remind me again: why does a professed psychic need a cell phone?) There are myriad soi-disant advisors out there. They are not within my purview here.

So that leaves us with two quite common and confused interventions that merit some discussion and separation: coaching and mentoring.

I've done both, and I still do. I maintain a global mentoring program and have instructed "mentor masters" in how best to help others. Thus, it's been important for me to understand the differences.

A *mentor* who is within an organization is usually a superior to whom the person being mentored does not report. Mentors are usually in an entirely different hierarchy. Such mentors are common in larger organizations, which may have formal mentor programs. Generally, high-potential people are assigned a mentor to help them overcome cultural, political, and ethical issues that they may encounter. Such mentoring can also be informal and virtually accidental. In police departments, a mentor is often called a "rabbi" who looks after the well-being of someone whom he has taken under his wing.

Outside of an organization, mentors often provide help to entrepreneurs, owners of small firms, and professional services providers. This is a one-on-one relationship that may be formalized or completely informal.

If it is informal, we hear phrases such as, "Peter Drucker was a true mentor to me when I became involved with assisting clients with their strategies." That statement does not imply a formal relationship or even a personal connection. It means that the individual was motivated, guided, and/or informed by Drucker's works.

If it is formal, we hear, "I was mentored by Maria Gomez," meaning that the individual had a personal relationship with the mentor, most probably, although not necessarily, for money. (I sometimes have to gently nudge people who claim that they were mentored by me because they've read some of my books or attended some workshops, since that implies inclusion in my formal program. I can't allow that claim for quality and branding reasons.)

Stop It! Don't use mentor *and* coach *interchangeably. Not only does doing so unduly cloud the two functions, but if you encourage prospects to do that, you may be lowering your potential fees. Read on!*

Here are some clear distinctions between coaches and mentors:

Attribute	Coaches	Mentors
Initiative	As often proactive as reactive	Solely reactive
Scope	May work with groups	Works only with individuals
Duration	Set tenure with disengagement	Open-ended/retainer
Key feature	Periodic interaction	Accessibility
Proximity	Tough to do solely remotely	Easy to do remotely
Fees	Based on value to the client	Retainer for access
Accountability	Guiding development	Sounding board

Attribute	Coaches	Mentors
Focus of expertise	Heavy process, some content	Can be either
Primary client	Organizational	Entrepreneurial
Specialties	Unfortunately, yes	Irrelevant
Experience	Needn't have done the job	Must have done the job
Ease of entry	Simple	Tougher (earned)

As a rule, mentors are experienced, successful people who provide wisdom and insights that may or may not require actual content expertise in the subject matter. Coaches, however, generally need strong process skills and some demonstrable knowledge of the content involved. (*Content* is what is being discussed; *process* is how you do what is discussed. Manufacturing tires is a content issue, but decision making is a process that transcends the content of the subject matter.)

The segmentation into "life coaches" and so forth has always struck me as more than silly. What qualifies someone to be a life coach, even if you can conjure up a definition? Would it be someone who has already lived life and can therefore provide empirical advice? Or someone who is now living such an unequivocally great life that others can only gawk in envy? I find that most life coaches are so pretentious that they need to, well, get a life.

Before you howl, I know that athletic coaches are a different sort, and that financial coaches focus on one bit of content—points conceded. But you're reading this to enter the field of, or vastly improve your success in, professional coaching. So it's vital that you understand the mainstream and not worry about the peripheral. (My personal trainer may be coaching me, but he refers to himself as a personal trainer, and my financial guy calls himself a financial strategist. I've never heard my lawyer refer to himself as a legal coach.)

There are grand and quite fundamental reasons why people require coaches, and we'll talk about them next. You may find flaws with some of my distinctions between coaches and mentors, or you may come up with a dozen more differences. No matter. What I want to convey is that coaching is a noble and important profession in its own right, need not be further specialized or delimited, and never need be apologized for.

No matter what the field, great coaches share a passion for improving their clients' condition. Often as not, that requires restraint, not forcefulness. I'll use a sports coach as an example: Joe McCarthy, the legendary New York Yankees baseball manager, once remarked to a reporter during batting practice that the future Hall of Fame player Mel Ott had the most perfect swing he'd ever seen.

"What did he say when you pointed that out?" asked the reporter.

"Oh, I'd never tell him," said McCarthy, "or I'd make him self-conscious and he'd begin thinking about it."

Mentors don't have to worry about this crucial distinction, but coaches do: the decision whether to leave someone alone in unconscious competency, bring them into conscious competency, or move them from the latter into the former is one of the most telling attributes of successful coaches. When a mentor is approached, the conversation is almost always about conscious competency.

But the true coach has the opportunity and the responsibility to deal with so much more than that.

THE (SURPRISING) REASONS THAT WE REQUIRE COACHES

Coaching has been around forever because it's been needed forever. We're not talking about some ephemeral improvement, like treading on hot coals or power meditation. People need to be coached for the following reasons:

- They identify a need.
  - They consistently fail at something.
  - They want to be part of the "in crowd" (normative pressure).
  - They want an excuse. ("Even my coach can't help me.")
  - They want to get better for future benefit.
- Someone else identifies a need.
  - They are unconsciously causing problems.
  - They are part of common programs (everyone at this level is coached).
  - They have been identified for advancement.
- Their conditions and needs change.
  - They are "made redundant."
  - They decide to change companies or careers.
  - They need new skills and behaviors.
  - They must master new techniques (e.g., technology).
- The problem is that nothing has changed.
  - They don't know what they don't know (recent graduates).
  - They won't be successful unless they receive the coaching that others are receiving.
- There is an innate human desire to improve.
  - They want to get better at their passions (bass fishing, making love).
  - They are bored with their current condition.

- They seek assurance that they're not missing anything.
- They want to compete (gamblers, contestants).
- They want to brag and improve their ego gratification.
• They are themselves coaches, trainers, or teachers.
- They need to remain on the leading edge of the process.
- They need to create excellent role models.
- They are their own laboratory.
• They seek to validate their worth and success.
- They want to avoid complacency, even though they are "on top."
- They require external validation to prove their worth.
- They lack other kinds of support networks and feedback options.

With that kind of need, how can you not make it in this profession?!

I admit that some of these needs may be overlapping, but they're worth considering for your own skill development and marketing plans. Here are some practical examples:

1. Beauty contestants and spelling bee competitors are no longer able to win based on their native skills, talents, or beauty. They don't stand a chance unless they are carefully coached on technique, fatigue, judging, and so forth. When I was a contestant on the game show *Jeopardy*, doing it as a lark between business trips, I was astounded to see, after the

preliminary qualifiers, that all my fellow contestants were studying and practicing. It's like being a good schoolyard athlete (which I was): it's not enough for the big time. (I lost in the first round to a dancing waiter from Iowa.)

2. SAT coaching became big business when so much emphasis came to be placed on these tests for college admissions. Despite the deemphasis lately, we see people being coached for success in standardized tests all over the world. One of my clients does nothing but help prepare people to pass the bar exam, often with the law schools' recommendations and blessings.

3. Just as you shouldn't serve as your own lawyer even if you are one, you should never serve as your own coach. I routinely help time management experts with time management, marketing gurus with marketing, and sales top guns with sales. We make our own worst clients, and good people need sounding boards.

> *Stop It! Never think of coaching as being strictly remedial or in response to weakness. The best and the brightest use coaches to avoid complacency.*

4. Superiors often require external validation. A board may demand that senior executives be coached not because they are failing, but because they are doing so well. The enlightened attempt here is to ensure that top people are continually challenged and their abilities stretched. When I coached the CEO of a major drug company, who was superb, he asked at the end of our engagement if I thought he could serve as the CEO of a couple of larger pharmaceutical

companies that were also my clients. I assured him that he could. But he needed that assurance, just as the board needed to know that he was on top of his game.

5. The very best performers you can think of usually have strong relationships with coaches. Athletes, entertainers, business executives, executive directors, hoteliers, restaurateurs—the best of the best frequently ensure their continued success by constantly being challenged. When the competition isn't close, top performers need some other stimulation and urgency to create still higher levels of performance. As a client at Hewlett-Packard told me, "We hire consultants not because we're not doing well, but because we're wary of solely breathing our own exhaust." The same holds true for individuals and coaches. As Satchel Paige said: "Don't look back, someone may be gaining on you."

6. There are simply too many "yes men" around. If you want trenchant feedback, you need someone whose retirement plan is not vested in the organization, and who isn't lobbying for someone else's corner office. Politicians are notorious for listening to the wrong people, those who tell them only what they want to hear, and consequently they do terribly in debates or manage to mangle every sound bite. That's why top political coaches, like James Carville and Mary Matalin (husband and wife on different sides of the aisle), are in such demand and are so expensive. They give honest advice, and they aren't looking for a plum job in the next administration.

Coaching is not a special event, it's an ongoing dynamic in personal and professional growth. That is a key mindset to retain as you read this book, especially the marketing and fee sections. You are not introducing a special, infrequent intervention, like a five-year medical checkup, a round-the-world trip, or orthodontia. You're creating a relationship that is normal and an ongoing part of someone's growth. That doesn't mean that your coaching is infinite, but it can be periodic.

It also means that, just as there is no shame in going to the dentist and there is a reward for attending a business convention (or an opera), coaching is a desirable and rewarding experience. You cannot position it as remedial and reactive to performance deviations, although at times it will be. You must position it as a sign of confidence, investment, and strength. Organizations don't invest in people who they don't value.

Finally, let's look at the consequences of not being coached (just as people view not going to the dentist, not getting out of the house, or not eating the right foods, which are ongoing conversations):

- What worked years ago doesn't work any more, yet the individual still clings to the outdated methods, wondering what's wrong with "today's customer" or "young employees" or "this economy."
- The competition readily gains a march, while the individual simply gets better and better at what he or she is already sufficiently good at.
- An insularity and isolation grows, and there is a tropism toward those who readily agree, further segregating the individual and/or the organization.
- It's exceedingly tough to be a coach yourself. Consulting expert Edgar Schein once said, "If you want to understand something, try to teach it." I would add, "If you want to help others understand it,

try coaching them." But it's tough to do that if you yourself haven't served as the exemplar and experienced the process.

- You're never able to fully capitalize on success. We prepare for failure, but we seldom adequately plan for success. We fear trouble, but we don't exult in opportunity. Without coaching, we're often blind to what we need to do after we've succeeded. We lose leverage and momentum.

- We don't gain "best practices" and external baselines for success, and we tend to miss the future, or to respond much later than others. We need external stimuli if we are to shine.

If those aren't enough reasons to understand why coaches are so valuable and are needed by so many people, then I don't know how else to convince you, and I suggest that you may want to put down this book and go into another line of work. It's not enough for you to realize that there is "need." You have to integrate how vital you are to others' well-being, and the tremendous value you provide to both individuals and organizations, and to their personal as well as professional lives.

WHY GREAT ATHLETES USUALLY AREN'T GREAT COACHES

Throughout history, the occasions when a great athlete has become a great coach have been relatively rare. Vince Lombardi, the deified Green Bay Packers coach, was a decent football player at Fordham, nothing more. Walter Alston, who managed baseball's Dodgers for over 20 years, appeared at bat in the major leagues just once, and struck out. Whether it's soc-cer or ice skating or hockey, the pattern is the same.[2]

Furthermore, when we look at some examples that defy my thesis—say, Bill Russell, the amazing Boston Celtics bas-ketball center who also coached the team to championships (as did a former point guard, K.C. Jones)—I would tell you that my German shepherd could have coached that team to victory, so laden was it with talent.[3] However, one of the great coaches of all time, with one of the greatest winning percentages ever, was Red Auerbach, a short, out-of-shape, cigar-smoking genius.

Great athletes use coaches. Tiger Woods (one of the great golfers in history, despite his peccadilloes) uses coaches for his swing and his putting. Greg Louganis, one of history's great-est divers, used an assortment of coaches. All professional teams carry on their rosters, at significant expense, coaches who specialize in everything from strength and conditioning to kicking angles.

That's because even the best need constant tune-ups and even occasional remedial work. It's also because championship form is voluble, and what worked yesterday may not work so well tomorrow against new competition, with muscles that are slightly older or game strategies that have evolved.

People need coaches who are proficient and adept at some aspect of what they seek to do. A world-class skier doesn't need another world-class skier to help her emerge more quickly from the starting gate, but she does require a coach who knows how to create quick starts and anticipate the clock. The same rela-tionship applies to business and to you, as a coach.

---

[2] Yes, I know you can cite an exception here and there, but that's what circumscribes my rule.

[3] John Havlicek, Sam Jones, Don Nelson, Tom Sanders, and Larry Siegfried, to name a few.

> *Stop It!* **You *don't have to be better than the person being coached at what he or she is seeking to do.* You merely have to be adept enough at some aspect of it to improve the person's condition.**

A client of mine is an expert in small legal firms. He has a ton of intellectual property, including books, videos, audio, workshops, and so on. But he is primarily a coach to owners and managing partners who are seeking to increase the firm's value, or merge, or acquire, or improve revenues. (He doesn't bill himself specifically as a "coach," which is the point of this chapter.)

However, he has had periodic self-esteem crises, which ultimately erupted in, of all things, a workshop I was conducting on self-esteem.

"I've never actually been a law firm managing partner," he noted morosely, "so where do I get the chutzpah[4] to advise these people?"

I asked him to respond to these questions:

- Do you have a major body of work on the subject matter that's in the public domain? (He does.)
- Do you have a law degree? (He is an attorney, although nonpracticing.)
- Have you successfully advised managing partners on these issues, and have they paid you for your advice in accordance with your proposal? (He has a long, impressive track record and client list.)
- Is your name known in the field? (He has one of the strongest brands in his niche.)

---

[4] This is a technical, legal term meaning "judicial precedent."

- Do major trade associations in the profession have relationships with you? (Some publish his works; some have him speak to conferences; some co-sponsor his workshops.)
- Can you produce testimonials and references? (Readily.)
- Have you assembled best practices from your experiences successfully advising managing partners and their colleagues? (He has.)
- Do people approach you for help because you're known and respected? (They do.)

At that point, the rest of the group was groaning. This person had more experiences and content than any of the clients or prospects he would be working with. In other words, he didn't have to be, specifically, a managing partner. His skills, behaviors, and experiences were better than those of a managing partner for what his intent was in coaching people to better performance. In fact, no managing partner could match his positioning to do just that.

But he had to realize that. The first sale is always to yourself.

If you review my bullet list of questions to my client, you may not (in fact, probably do not) possess as many assets as he does. But you have many of them, and you can readily develop the others. You don't have to be a better performer at the job your client does; you have to be better at certain components of it that you can use to improve the client's condition.

I have never been the CEO of a Fortune 1000 firm, but I certainly have been a successful coach of many of them. I've never served as executive director of a nonprofit, but I've advised a slew of them who have improved significantly as a result of my intervention. You and I are actually better off and better positioned to coach other than the "star athletes."

Stars in their field generally don't make great coaches themselves because

- Their behavioral set is quite different. They are used to breaking rules, taking risks, standing out, and getting the ball in pressure situations. A coach can't act that way.
- They are highly competitive, and their strong egos often "spill over" from confidence into arrogance.[5]
- They are driven, direct, and eager, and they want to act rapidly.
- While they play on a team, they are not the exemplars for teamwork.
- They love the personal adulation and seek the roar of the crowd.
- They believe that it's easier to get forgiveness than to get permission.
- They generally want instant gratification.
- They don't like compromise and prefer their way, not a collaborative way.
- They talk a lot and don't listen well.

Obviously, I'm painting with a broad brush. But if you look at the summary of skills, behaviors, and experiences earlier in this chapter, you'll find that they are not exactly the hallmarks of superstars.

---

[5] Working definitions:

Confidence: The honest belief that you can help others to learn.
Arrogance: The honest belief that you have nothing left to learn yourself.
(*Smugness:* Arrogance without the talent.)

The mentor model works better for the star athletes in organizations. It is reactive and uses personal experiences and contacts to help resolve issues that are presented. But the coaching model is far less appropriate, with its needs to be proactive, establish behavioral objectives, and observe and listen carefully. Strong and "larger than life" leaders, whether George Patton or Jack Welch, weren't famous for their coaching skills. Their chains of command took care of subordinate development.

SUMMARY

Most consultants, advisors, counselors, and those in helping professions are already coaches. Coaching is something that is within your repertoire, not "who you are." You may choose to focus exclusively on it, but the more you know about behavior, organizational dynamics, change management, feedback and evaluation, and so on, the better you'll be as a coach.

Certifications don't matter, because there is no accepted discipline or approved regimen for coaching. Your ability to create a body of work and become adept at components of what your clients need will be crucial. Hence, age, gender, culture, and other irrelevant factors are to be ignored.

There are many more reasons for the need for coaches than people suspect. The overarching requirement, however, is to improve the client's condition. Let's move now to how that's assessed and accomplished, and discuss the business of coaching.

THE COACH'S CALLING

YOU'RE NOBODY TILL SOMEBODY WANTS YOU

IMPROVING THE CLIENT'S CONDITION

I've been discussing the concept of improving the client's condition throughout the first chapter, so let's take some time to ensure that we're all clear about this concept.

Here are some keys to guide you in your orientation toward the business:

1. You do not conduct business with "entities." GE may be a client, and you may be working within the area known as a call center, but someone has purchased your services and somebody constitutes your prospective buyer. We conduct business with humans, not with bricks and mortar.

2. The economic buyer is the person who can write a check. This is not to be confused with feasibility buyers, which are usually lodged in human resources and are often assigned the responsibility for finding

"vendors" for coaching assignments. (At the conclusion of this chapter, we'll deal with specific techniques for determining who the buyer is and circumventing the rest.) The economic buyer is the one you want to please, the one who may rehire you, provide testimonials, serve as a reference, and so forth. That's the person whom you want to find, delight, and nurture.

3. The reason you're being hired is to improve someone's performance. That's always an output or result. The input (coaching, testing, observing, and so on) is useless and unimportant if the output isn't improved. That improvement has to be manifest, evident, and apparent. For example, the person's "feeling better" doesn't matter if the performance is not affected positively.

4. There is a finite time frame, relatively short-term for the business and infinitely minuscule in terms of the cosmos, in which to accomplish this improvement. That must be set, at least within a reasonable range, at the outset.

5. There is often pain in improvement, as in working out with a trainer or studying for a midterm exam. You aren't there to be loved; you're there to help someone else improve. You are not there to be validated. Patients pay the therapist, not the other way around.

Stop It! Never assume that your client is damaged. That's a disastrous way to begin. Even if you're told that, validate others' opinions through your own observations.

The major issue you face with your client is the difference between your buyer and your client. Sometimes they are one and the same, sometimes not.

Your buyer—the person writing the check—may want your personal coaching assistance for himself. That would remain between the two of you, so there's not much of a problem there.

But your buyer may be writing you a check to coach someone else, most probably a subordinate. If that's the case, you have some issues to resolve; they include

- What is the nature of the confidentiality? Are you to observe strict confidence with the client, or is the buyer entitled to know? If the latter, then the actual client must be informed of this. You can't allow your client to infer that interactions are confidential when, in fact, they are not meant to be.
- Will the buyer participate directly in the process? Will he or she be present during feedback, offer independent feedback, ask you to add to your comments, and so forth? What, exactly, is the buyer's role?
- Who will set the developmental objectives? Will the buyer do it alone or with the client? If the former, who will inform the client, and will the client buy in voluntarily or have no choice?
- What will be the metrics for success and how will
  - You know they've been reached (or not)?
  - The client know they've been reached?
  - The buyer know they've been reached?
- If there is disagreement among the three of you, how will you resolve the issues? What evidence and/or behavior will be used?

- Who will decide to disengage when success is reached or when it is deemed that success can't be reached? Who makes that final decision?
- Who will evaluate your performance: the buyer, the client, or both?
- What is the frequency of your reporting to the buyer if that is desired, and who initiates such reporting?
- Do any other parties have the right to receive progress reports and debriefings?

These issues must be resolved prior to the submission of a proposal. You can't afford to allow the client to have the misconception that the work is confidential when it's not, or the buyer to assume that he or she can interfere at any time when that wasn't the agreement. The rules can't change in midstream unless everyone agrees to it, and that is seldom a good idea. It's eremitic to believe that coaching takes place in a vacuum. Unless you're meeting off-site and in disguise, word inevitably gets out. So it's imperative that you have the rules of the road established before the trip commences.

We'll discuss this phenomenon further when we tackle fees, but note in Figure 2-1 that there are two concurrent benefits that accrue to clients and buyers from your coaching. One is the importance of the result to the individual, and the other is the importance of the results to the organization. Both are usually present, but they either are not equal or are not perceived to be equal. Your greatest contribution and value is when you can accomplish both, and they are clearly manifest.

Another way to view this relationship is shown in Figure 2-2.

If you simply coach the "public" without an organizational connection, you'll always be in the upper left quadrant. If you merely contract through training or HR, you'll inevitably be in the bottom left. If the buyer is not your client and his or her

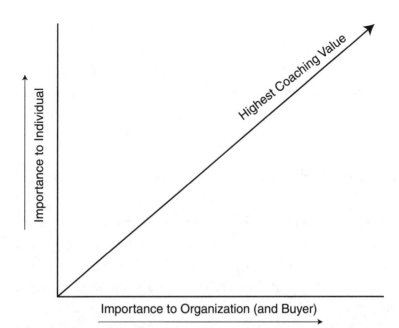

Figure 2-1   Maximum Coaching Value

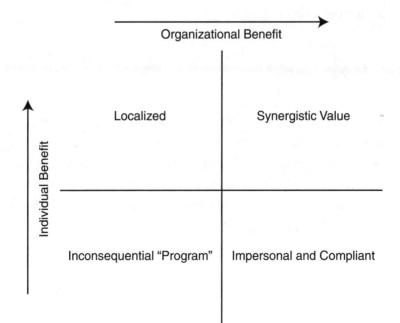

Figure 2-2   Comparing Individual and Organizational Benefits

subordinates are forced into coaching, you'll have compliance but seldom commitment, in the lower right column.

In both graphics depicting your potential value, you want to migrate to the upper right. You do that by developing trust with the buyer and the client.

DEVELOPING TRUST

Once you orient yourself to dealing with true buyers—people who can write a check for your value—you have to begin that journey by establishing trust. Ironically, the longer you take to establish the relationship, the faster you'll obtain high-quality business.

The reason that trust is so important is that the buyer is not going to readily share developmental objectives and related information with you if he or she doesn't trust you. Let's define trust for our purposes:

> Trust is my firm belief that you have my best interests in mind.

If I trust you, I'll listen to "pushback" and critique and consider it as constructively intended. If I don't trust you, I'll be skeptical of even compliments and accolades because I'll be wondering about a possible hidden agenda.

How can you tell whether or not you have trust, which may take 10 minutes to establish with some people and a series of meetings with others? Here are some indicators:

- The buyer offers information that you didn't request, such as, "There have been some poor management decisions from the parent company."

- The buyer asks your opinion: "What would you recommend in terms of starting with one person or the entire team?"
- The buyer extends the time allotted to you to continue the conversation.
- Your questions are responded to with detail and precision.
- You are not asked for credibility sources (references, client lists, and so on).
- The buyer listens to your differing opinions about her positions and suggestions.
- There is no attempt to negotiate anything.

> *Stop It! Requesting help is not a sign of weakness, but of strength. We all need help. Asking for it is a healthy sign.*

Here's how you can accelerate the creation of trust.

ALAN'S TRUST BUILDERS

1. Offer ideas and value early. Don't be afraid to provide insights and suggestions. You want the buyer to think, "If I'm getting this much value from a first meeting, what would I get if I hired this person?!"
2. Base your comments on observed behavior and evidence, not suppositions or your own model. Example: "I've heard you say three times now that there is too much conflict between sales and R&D.

If I've heard that correctly, can you tell me why you think the conflict has reached this level?"

3. Never focus on your methodology or approaches. Focus on the buyer's goals and improved condition. Don't create a cairn of technology.

4. Try to focus on the "what," not the "how." Don't allow the buyer to advertently or inadvertently dictate an alternative to you, such as, "We need a 360-degree assessment of our top team."

5. Look successful. Don't take out a 99-cent pen to take notes. Use a Cartier or Mont Blanc. Wear a very good suit and accessories. Powerful people like to be around other powerful people.[1]

6. Do some homework. Find out something about the company, the division, its competitors, the individual you're meeting, and so forth. You don't have to become an expert, but you should be conversant. If you're in a bank, for instance, you should know what a loan defalcation is.

7. Drop into the conversation successful experiences and projects you've completed that you can talk about either specifically (with that party's permission, of course) or in a more general sense (JPMorgan Chase versus "a large financial institution").

8. Be well read. If the buyer mentions a play, or an article in the *Wall Street Journal* or the *Financial Times*, or a popular television show, it's helpful if you at least know of it.

---

[1] Absolutely and totally ignore anyone who tells you to "dumb down" your speech or attire with clients. These are weak and insecure people who want to drag you down to their own level of ineffectiveness.

9. Mind your manners. Practice business etiquette. Understand how to greet people and conduct yourself. (I suggest you never accept coffee or refreshments—they aren't needed, and they can create some serious damage.) Make sure your cell phone is turned off. Don't drag in 30 pounds of baggage.

In the "Trust Pyramid" I've created (see Figure 2-3), you can see that a referral from a peer is a strong source of trust. (Even the lower levels of this pyramid have high impact.) Manifest expertise would include intellectual property that the buyer is familiar with, which is why commercially published books are so powerful. Affiliative needs means that the buyer believes that you would "fit" well with his or her plans, the client, and/or the

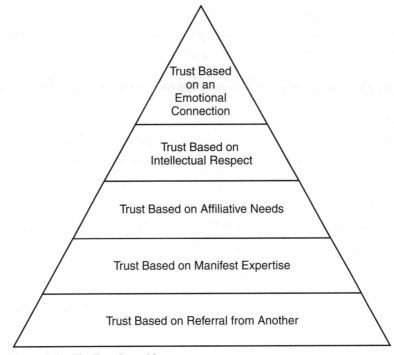

Figure 2-3   The Trust Pyramid

organization. Trust based on intellectual respect, which is that which you manifest in your conversations, is highly effective.

But trust that is emotionally based is the strongest of all, because logic makes us think, but emotion makes us act. The more you can establish an emotional bond—through empathy, common beliefs, courtesy, and so forth—the better off you'll be.

Note that, ideally, all of these sources, or at least several of them, are working for you at any one time. If you have none, then you are merely a vendor, not a partner, and at best you'll be relegated to the bowels of the organization, where nothing good ever happens.

ASSESSING PERFORMANCE AND PROGRESS

Unlike other forms of advising, coaching has distinct developmental objectives, as previously discussed, and it must include specific metrics for progress and success. You and the client (and, often, the buyer) must be able to agree on where you are relative to where you are supposed to be.

Moreover, improvement isn't important unless it's manifest. Although a variety of training people will cite four levels of measurement, they are (as usual) making the simple complex to try to create the impression of more sophistication than is justified. Unless there is a demonstrable improvement in performance, then what's the point? If I'm more confident, more self-assured, more motivated, and more self-reliant, yet none of those enviable traits are discernible in my actions, then why invest in their attainment?

The fall-down-laughing problem I had with EST (Erhart Seminars Training) 30 or so years ago was that the participants couldn't really describe how they were different, didn't appear to be any different, and urged that you had to attend the workshop to really understand the benefits (which wasn't so much a great developmental methodology as a slick marketing ploy). The same applies to treading on hot coals or rappelling down cliffs with "coaches." What's the discernable improvement I'll be seeing a month later? It's usually between nada and niente.[2]

The legendary training guru Bob Mager said it best: "How would you know it if you tripped over it?" Indeed.

Before you begin a coaching assignment—in fact, before you create the proposal—you must reach conceptual agreement with the buyer and the client (if they are different) about what indicators will be applied to determine success. That way, you can

- Adjust your pace.
- Provide assurances to the buyer, even if the client content is confidential.
- Make the client accountable for progress.
- Avoid disagreements about the rate of progress.
- Provide reinforcement through the attainment of mileposts.
- Expect others to also notice improvement and provide feedback.
- Provide for perpetuation of improvement after you disengage.

---

[2] Psychologists report that it's not unusual for them to treat the hot coal walkers later on, not for physical discomfort, but because what they were so proud of never carried over to their life and work. This is why no job description is big on perspiring feet.

Stop It! You have no idea about the success of your diet without a scale, or the speed of your vehicle without a speedometer, or the length of your speech without a timer. Don't try to help people improve without agreed-upon instrumentation.

You are the cicerone, the dragoman for your client. But you must transfer the skills and assess your client's progress collaboratively. Hence, how do you both know that improvement is underway and/or goals attained?

Here are some examples of poor metrics and improved metrics:

- You will feel more confident making public speeches and presentations. *Better:* Your hands will not shake, you will not need to hold your notes, and you will be able to take spontaneous questions from the audience.
- You will be more assertive in confronting conflict. *Better:* You will ask subordinates in conflict to calm down, ask each to recite his or her version of the disagreement in 60 seconds, then tell them whether they are arguing about objectives (goals) or alternatives (routes). They will both agree to return to you with a compromise within 24 hours.
- You will be confident of your subordinates' abilities to act independently. *Better:* You will stop cutting off subordinates' sentences in meetings, cease taking work from them because you can do it faster, and use those times when they fail to hold a brief evaluation session to help them learn what the error was.
- You will agree to get along with your spouse better and to respect your spouse's opinion. *Better:* You will

sit down each evening before dinner for 30 minutes to discuss your respective day's events, ask each other for advice, and say "thank you" after each piece of advice, whether it is used or not. Any humor or sarcasm that you express will be self-effacing and never directed at your partner.

You get the idea. You can see the better statements in the environment. They are dispositive and evidentiary. You can recognize them if you trip over them.

Another way to view metrics is that they measure outputs, not inputs, not deliverables, not attitudes. Take a look at this sequence:

Beliefs

Attitudes

Behaviors

We normally "whack" behaviors that are inappropriate or ineffective. We tend to take coercive action. We address "inappropriate attitudes" through normative pressure—join the "in crowd"; here's what all the "best" people are doing.

But only by changing beliefs—through an appeal to the client's self-interest—do we achieve commitment and not merely compliance. During Prohibition, there were more speakeasies in New York than there had been legal bars prior to it. That's because no one believed that drinking was bad for them, and coercion was ineffective. But the smoking rates have been drastically cut because of appeals to health, seeing one's grandchildren, secondhand adverse effects, and other educational reasons that strike the belief system.

Only behaviors are seen. Consequently, you know you're effective at changing beliefs (and have the correct appeal to self-interest) only if you're able to measure the difference: the individual stops smoking, tobacco sales are reduced, public areas are legally smoke-free, and so forth.

Many clients will tell you that they've changed: that they are happy, or fulfilled, or no longer stressed, or that they can flap their wings and fly. You don't believe that last claim, but why would you believe any of the others without proof based on behavior and evidence? Talk is cheap. Claims are easy. Behaving differently is difficult.

That kind of change requires an outstanding coach, one who can give accurate, empathetic, and candid feedback.

PROVIDING ACCURATE, COMPASSIONATE, BUT CANDID FEEDBACK

There are two kinds of feedback in this world: solicited and unsolicited. Some people claim that the only thing to do with any feedback is to listen to it, but these are the masochists who also believe that flossing is ordained by God and that Piers Morgan is a celebrity.

Unsolicited feedback is always for the sender. Under the guise of helping you, he is stroking his own ego, trying to bring you down to his level, or simply playing passive-aggressive games. Fortunately, solicited feedback is that which the subject requests, and it is the heart and soul of coaching.

Providing feedback is a process. Even though great coaches seem to do it naturally, it has clear characteristics, which we can deconstruct here.

ALAN'S FABULOUS
FEEDBACK FEATURES

- *Planned and unplanned.* You should have scheduled feedback sessions with your client, but also feel free to provide feedback extemporaneously and immediately when it will be most effective.

- *Positive and negative.* All feedback in coaching should be constructive, which means that it includes both the negative to be improved and the positive to be reinforced.

- *Empathetic, not sympathetic.* It's critical to understand what your client is feeling, but not to feel what he is feeling. Sympathy provides commiseration, but empathy provides growth.

- *Timely.* Telling someone what she did yesterday or last week is not nearly as effective as telling that person what she has just done.

- *Focused on improvable points.* Telling someone to write more clearly on an easel is valid; telling him that he should switch from the left hand to the right is not.

- *Her, not you.* Telling someone how you do it is not as effective as using third parties and other, observable examples. The client can always rationalize, "Well, you're the coach; of course you can do it well," but she can't use that logic when she sees peers performing at the desired level.

- *Tell and listen.* Counterintuitively, you must listen to your client's reactions prior to, during, and after the feedback. There may be circumstances and observations from the client that influence the validity of your own observations.

- *Differentiate the channel.* Some feedback is best provided in discussion, especially when interaction is important; some is best done in writing, when you want to reinforce and document; some is best done in front of others, some privately; some in person, some by phone. Choose the best medium for the circumstances.

- *Focus on the facts.* Feedback is based on observed behavior and evidence. Telling someone that he doesn't appear to be a "team player" is rather worthless, especially compared to, "You're late for every scheduled meeting by at least 10 minutes."

- *Demonstrate impact.* Don't just cite the evidence, but also explain the positive or negative impact created for the client and others involved. The repercussions and results dramatize the need to change or reinforce.

Aside on Feedback

I had just delivered a keynote speech to a wonderful ovation in Birmingham, England. I was ushered into a reception, where I was asked by a speech coach (who else?) if he could give me feedback.

"Is there anything in what's left of the British Empire that could stop you?" I inquired. He totally ignored that, being the good listener that he is.

"When you move about the stage, I can't focus on your points," he pedantically noted, "but when you stand still, I can pick up every point. Do you know what that's called?"

"Yes." I assured him. "A learning disability."

While providing feedback spontaneously is very effective, you nevertheless have to pick your moments. You shouldn't do it when you are rushing down a hall, or right before a major meeting, or from a speeding car. That's because there are the potential impediments to the feedback loop shown in Figure 2-4.

You and I (and any two or more people) have differing factors that "color" and influence our understanding—our ability to "get" what the other person intends. There are two types of interference:

1. *Environmental.* Don't attempt to communicate important feedback in a crowd, where there are distractions, or where your client might not focus. When you and/or your client are taking cell phone calls and checking e-mail, not much interpersonal feedback is going to be exchanged or digested.

2. *Cognitive.* This one is trickier, because it's hidden. You must test for understanding, to ensure that what you mean is what the other person "gets" and that what he or she means is what you "get." Example: "If you agree that you need to allow for your

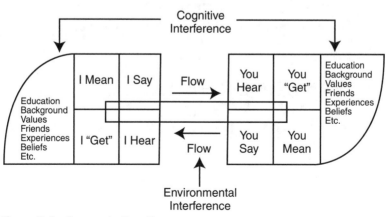

Figure 2-4   Communications Flow

subordinates' self-evaluation before giving them your own, how might you change the next review session?" By asking for an example of application, you're testing to ensure that the proper message was received in the proper manner.

Stop It! Never use satire or sarcasm in feedback, and be sure that anything that might be ambiguous is given in person, not by e-mail or even by phone. "Nice job" can take on many different meanings in writing when there is no inflection or body language associated with it— particularly if your client has low self-esteem.

Your obligation to your client goes well beyond "first, do no harm." It is to take every step possible to ensure that the developmental objectives agreed upon are met, according to the metrics you have established to inform both of you. You don't need to appear gnomic, simply sincere and honest. That requires frequent and candid feedback, compassionate but often brutally honest. Coaching is a profession; it's not a social undertaking to make friends, seek approval, and be loved.

If those are your overriding concerns, get a dog.

DETERMINING THE TRUE BUYER (AND WHY THE BUYER IS NEVER IN HR)

Your buyer may be the client or may be someone who is obtaining your services for someone who works for him or her. Buyers sign checks (or can authorize the computer to produce one).

Human Resources (HR) is often called upon to broker the services of vendors. It vets people who provide commodity services or products. Its wholly invented but favorite phrase for this is apparently being "tasked" to perform a certain function.

You are neither a vendor nor a commodity.

With rare exception, HR and training departments do not have budgets. They merely represent someone else. The final decision is seldom theirs. In any case, you must meet the buyer and the client personally so that you can determine if the chemistry is correct, the expectations reasonable, and the environment conducive to improvement. While there are infrequent instances of a senior HR officer having a budget and authority, if you work through Human Resources, 90 percent of the time you will find yourself in the La Brea Tar Pits of organizational life.[3]

Here is how you can determine who the economic buyer is.

ALAN'S QUESTIONS TO IDENTIFY TRUE BUYERS

1. Whose budget will support this initiative?

2. Who can immediately approve this project?

3. To whom will people look for support, approval, and credibility?

4. Who controls the resources required to make this happen?

5. Who has initiated this request?

[3] Lest you think that I'm being too critical of HR, name me three top HR executives who, in the past 10 years, were promoted to the CEO spot in a Fortune 500 firm. You can't. You can find general counsels, vice presidents, actuaries, and even outsiders, but not top HR people. There is a reason for that.

6. Who will claim responsibility for the results?

7. Who will be seen as the main sponsor and/or champion?

8. Do you have to seek anyone else's approval?

9. Who will accept or reject proposals?

10. If you and I were to shake hands, could I begin tomorrow?

Key Point: The larger the organization, the greater the number of economic buyers. They need not be the CEO or the owner, but they must be able to authorize and produce payment. Committees are never economic buyers.

Stop It! Build your self-esteem to the point where you don't feel that you have to please everyone you stumble upon and are afraid that if you don't get the business, you'll starve. When you deal with people who can't say yes but can say no, guess what you'll always hear—NO!

In smaller organizations, the buyer is almost always the owner. In such cases, be aware that decisions can be more purely emotional. The owner may be deciding whether to invest in coaching or use the money for a son's orthodontia or a daughter's wedding. You don't find those kinds of factors intruding on decisions at Hewlett-Packard or Boeing.

Larger organizations have scores of buyers. One of my most important buyers in Merck had the title "Manager of International Development." You can't always tell a buyer by a business card (everyone in a bank is a vice president, for example), but you always can by a budget and the ability to spend it.

Buyers are interested in ROI—return on investment. If a buyer tells you that he has "sticker shock," what that buyer really means is that he doesn't see the appropriate return on the investment that he is being asked to make. Hence, the importance of objectives and metrics is joined by a third factor: value.

Value can be quantifiable (numbers and amounts of sales) or qualitative (less stress, higher repute). But in either case, it is valuable if it is developed with the buyer and is dramatic enough to justify the fees. Money is never about resources, but always about priorities. There is always money, but the buyer's key consideration is whether to give it to you rather than someone else!

The critical nuance is to develop the value with the buyer, so that there is commitment and conceptual agreement on the outcomes. That deed done, potential shock at fees is pretty much vitiated.

ALAN'S TECHNIQUES TO BUILD VALUE

1. What will these results mean for your organization?

2. How would you assess the actual return (ROI, ROA, ROS, ROE, or some other metric)?

3. What would be the extent of the improvement (or correction)?

4. How will these results affect the bottom line?

5. What are the annualized savings (the first year might be deceptive)?

6. What is the intangible impact (e.g., on repute, safety, or comfort)?

7. How would you, personally, be better off or better supported?

8. What is the scope of the impact (on customers, employees, vendors)?

9. How important is this compared to your overall responsibilities?

10. What if this fails?

Key Point: Subjective value (stress alleviated) can be every bit as important as more tangible results (higher sales). Never settle for, "Don't worry, it's important." Find out how important, because that will dictate the acceptable fee range.

Also, ask yourself these questions: why me, why now, why in this manner?

If you are among the few people who can coach in these circumstances (you're local, you're from the industry, you've written a book on the issues), you're more valuable. If there is an urgency, a critical event approaching, or a limited window of opportunity, you are more valuable. If the client has tried this before, perhaps internally, and been unsuccessful, then you are more valuable.

The answers to the previous questions and these added three dimensions will give you a very solid understanding of your worth to the client.

Then add two more dimensions: professional and personal. There will be benefits that accrue to the organization, but also to the individual. They may be skewed one way or the other, or they may affect both equally. No matter. Both are valuable.

Your ability to extract these conclusions about value creates conceptual agreement with the client, including performance objectives, measures of success, and value to the organization and the individual. You also create a case for why you may be even more valuable than others in fulfilling the goals.

Now you're ready for the next step. Having found potential success, you want to ensure that it happens.

SETTING YOURSELF UP FOR SUCCESS

HOW TO STACK THE DECK IN YOUR FAVOR

FINALIZING CONCEPTUAL AGREEMENT

No matter what you believe or don't believe (or I've already persuaded you) about coaching, this is immutable: it is a business.

If you consider it a "calling" or a "duty" or your "life's work," that's all well and good, but you're talking about an avocation, not an occupation. An avocation is a hobby, pastime, or interest that absorbs your time and energy, provides you with gratification, may or may not involve helping others, and does not have a direct bearing on your financial well-being (although it could undermine it). An occupation is a career that provides the financial sustenance to support your lifestyle and fuel your future.

They may be congruent. But if they are not, or if you act solely on the basis of an avocation without an additional occupation, there is a name we attach to the phenomenon: failure.

> *Stop It! Real wealth is discretionary time. Money is simply fuel for your life. You can always make another dollar, but you can't make another minute. Don't let the pursuit of money erode your wealth.*

Consequently, you must behave as a businessperson. You are a professional coach (consultant) who has a business. My brand is my name, and also terms such as *Million Dollar Consultant*® and *The Contrarian*, and I produce immense amounts of intellectual property for a wide variety of clients. But underlying all of that is my legal entity, Summit Consulting Group, Inc. That's because my value and my clients and my future are all within the framework of proper business methods.

Figure 3-1 shows the schematic of what your approach to your prospects should be.

The "shared values" aren't spiritual or religious, but rather business values. For example, you and the client should share beliefs about confidentiality, or investing in top performers, or removing people who can't be developed, or whatever it is that is critical to the project. The relationship is then built on the trust we discussed in Chapter 2.

Conceptual agreement is the mutual understanding of the objectives (developmental outcomes of the coaching), metrics (indicators of progress and/or completion), and value (the impact of the results on the individual and the organization). Progressing to this point will result in better than 80 percent of your proposals being accepted, and the implementation that follows will produce the expected results, which in turn will reinforce the relationship (we accomplished what we agreed we would).

Thus, this is a partnership between you and the buyer, whether the buyer is also your client or whether someone else

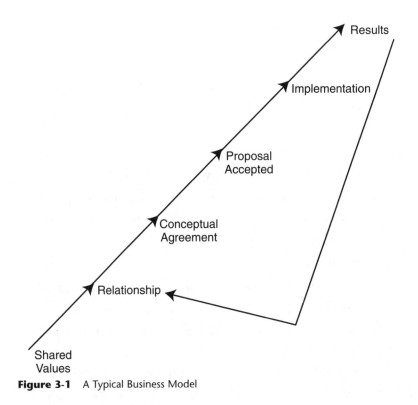

Figure 3-1   A Typical Business Model

or some others are the clients. That's why trying to work through intermediaries such as Human Resources is folly. This is a relationship business, so trying to form relationships with the wrong people or through other people is doomed to failure.

Similarly, if you try to "leap" up that chart, you're heading for trouble. Submitting a proposal without conceptual agreement from the economic buyer—who alone has the fiduciary responsibility for investing and evaluating ROI—is an exercise in futility, as is trying to create conceptual agreement with someone who does not yet trust you.

The sequence is simple but vital.

To ensure that you submit a proposal that is likely to be accepted, follow these guidelines:

1. Find and meet with the economic buyer. If you're meeting with someone else, particularly a gatekeeper or an intermediary, don't establish a strong relationship, but use that contact to reach the economic buyer. More than 50 percent of failures to secure coaching business result from ignoring this step because of fear of offending a low-level person or fear of meeting a high-level person.

2. Develop a trusting relationship. This may take more than one meeting. Never end a meeting without a definitive next step, including time, date, and accountability.

3. Establish objectives, measures, and value, and make sure that the buyer commits to them (conceptual agreement). These should all come from the buyer, through your adept questioning and persistence. Steps 2 and 3 account for another 30 percent of the failure to get business. Coaches are too willing to "pitch" rather than discuss, and they don't bother getting agreement on the value of the project, and hence, don't have strong ROI propositions. Never discuss fees at this early point, only outcomes.

4. Submit a proposal[1] that incorporates all of this, along with joint accountabilities, timing, and fees. Ideally, the proposal should have options, which we'll discuss later in this chapter. This is the first time the buyer should see the fees. (If you're discussing fees and not

---

[1] For detailed help on proposals, see my book *How to Write a Proposal That's Accepted Every Time* or go to the downloads for this book for samples. In brief, a proposal has nine steps: Situation Appraisal, Objectives, Measures of Success, Value, Options and Methodology, Timing, Joint Accountabilities, Terms and Conditions, and Acceptance.

value before this point in your dealings with the buyer, you've lost control of the discussion.)

5. Submit the proposal with a clear follow-up discussion date, for example, Tuesday at 10 a.m. Eastern. At that time, you ask the buyer which option is preferred.

6. Collect your deposit or fee and begin the project.

My experience over the last 25 years has been that this simple sequence will multiply your chances of proposal acceptance exponentially. You may submit fewer proposals, but you'll close many more of them.

CREATING RULES OF ENGAGEMENT

Your coaching project will have a starting date and an eventual ending date (which might be a range, such as 60–90 days). That's the easy part. It's what happens during the project that gets tricky.

So before we discuss how you'll coach (the methodologies), let's take a look at the conditions under which you'll coach (the process). I've chosen to call these the "rules of engagement," although they could as easily be called "criteria" or "dynamics" or "interactions."

1. Accessibility
   - Will access to you be only while you're with the client, or will it also be by e-mail, phone, and fax? Will it be during the client's business hours, your business hours (if you are in different time zones), on weekends, in the evenings? If you don't create accurate expectations, you could find yourself with

your cell phone ringing on your way to dinner on Saturday night!

- How many people have access? Are you coaching an individual or a team? Does the buyer have access if the buyer is not the client?
- What about emergencies, abrupt challenges, harsh feedback, and so forth?
- What is the expected response time? Is it within 90 minutes, or a half-day, or 24 hours, or a week?

2. Confidentiality

- If the buyer is not the client, is what feedback the buyer is entitled to or seeking crystal clear, and does the client know it?
- Under what conditions will you break confidentiality or not grant it? Even priests and therapists will abrogate confidentiality when someone else may be in grave danger. More commonly, will you tell the proper authorities if you find out that theft is going on, or fraud?

> *Stop It! You can't regard confidentiality as sacrosanct. Here's a preventive action: Tell anyone who asks for confidentiality that you reserve the right to reveal what you learn or have been told if, in your sole judgment, it could do serious harm to the client or the organization. If that's not acceptable, then your client should not share the information with you.*

- What permanent record will there be? Are there physical or electronic notes, and, if so, where will they reside? Will they be destroyed at a given time? Who will have access? Can the client have copies? Can the buyer have copies?

- What is confidential that you, the coach, communicates? Can the client repeat what you state to others? Can anything that you provide in writing be revealed?

3. Elasticity

- What is the scope of the help? Does it extend to personal issues as well as professional ones, especially if they overlap?[2]

- If you're coaching both a team and its members, to what extent can you share feedback among individuals?

- Can you be asked to comment/advise on things beyond coaching, such as a decision that the team is trying to make or a problem that an individual is having that is not related to the developmental objectives?

- Can the assignment be postponed, delayed, or rescheduled? Can it be applied to other people who replace the person who was first named as the client? (These are never good practices in terms of momentum and continuity, but the issues do arise.)

- Will you give feedback to the buyer about peripheral elements, such as the quality of the meetings themselves that you attend, even though you're there to observe your client's behavior specifically?

---

[2] Be very careful, because you're probably not a licensed therapist, and, even if you are, business coaching and personal therapy should seldom, if ever, be combined in one resource.

Some of these rules of engagements may sound like obviousities, a neologism I've created to identify the blazingly apparent. But they need to be discussed. Too many coaches lose time, money, and energy because of two conditions:

1. *Scope creep.* This is the usually inadvertent and nonmalicious tendency for the client to increase requests and ask for additional services "while you're there," or "since we have access," or "because we need an objective resource and you're already working with us." Hewlett-Packard once called these "undocumented promises," meaning that people agreed to client requests that were nowhere to be found in the actual proposal.

2. *Scope seep.* This is an equally invidious phenomenon that I formally recognized and named about 10 years ago. In this case, the coach is inventing more work. You feel that you're merely a "hired hand," and so as long as you're on site or dealing with the client, you might also critique written documents, help with collecting receivables, and wash the trucks.

Both scope creep and scope seep are the results of low self-esteem. In the first case, you're afraid to say no because you're fearful of jeopardizing the engagement and goodwill. In the second, you're assertively trying to prove your worth because you feel like an imposter and must prevent the client from questioning the degree or merits of your contributions.

The first is reactive, the second proactive, and both are deadly in terms of expanding your work with no additional compensation, which is the definition of declining margins.

Rules of engagement should be established at the time of the proposal and reinforced once the project begins. They should be in writing. As you proceed with the project, you may want to amend them. If you're dealing with a team, make sure that everyone is on board. It's especially vital to understand what can and cannot be shared among team members. Each one is your client, so you can't have differing relationships and responses.

Finally, the rules of engagement have to include disengagement. There is an approximate completion date, which may be slightly altered as circumstances and progress dictate, and you may have debriefings and an occasional follow-up call or visit. But there comes a time when things are over.

Otherwise, you haven't created a coaching success so much as a codependency.

DETERMINING TIME FRAMES

How long is a coaching assignment? A coach once told me that he was going to be there "as long as he could convince the client he should stay."

How picaresque. That's not a coach. That's a parasite.

There are two basic dimensions to coaching time frames, so let's keep this simple.

Project

Here, you work on prescribed developmental objectives with metrics for success, and you depart when

- The objectives are achieved (presentations improve), or
- Sufficient progress has been made, and actual achievement is far in the future (preparing someone for promotion), or

- The objectives cannot be achieved (the client's skills, aptitudes, and/or behaviors are simply insufficient).

This is the most common form of coaching, and the disengagement is as important as the engagement. I haven't been kidding when I've said that we need to avoid codependency. The coach and the buyer need to decide when the progress is achieved, sufficient, or impossible (the three conditions given previously). When the buyer and the client are one and the same, it's incumbent on the coach to make the tough third call.

For any such assignment, you should have an intelligent estimate of the time required, which will include the buyer's consent and agreement. Since you should charge by the project and for value—and never for time[3]—it's imperative that you have a set time frame, even if it's a range.

> *Stop It! When you charge by the hour, you're establishing a conflict of interest, since the client is helped most by the quickest resolution, and the coach is helped most by the slowest. This is an antediluvian mentality. Stop charging by days and hours, and educate your buyers differently.*

As a rule, coaching assignments can be as brief as a few days or as long as a few months. You and the buyer should estimate a range (e.g., 30 to 45 days) based on factors such as these:

- Does the individual being coached travel or have a tough schedule?
- What other priorities have to be accommodated?

[3] Ethically, you never want to place the buyer in the position of having to make an investment decision every time he or she may need to access you.

- How much of a "convincing" or rapport period is necessary?
- How much testing and/or background work needs to be done?
- What's the urgency for improvement?
- What opportunities are there to practice and show improvement?
- Is it an individual, a small group, or a large team that's being coached?

In so doing, the two of you will develop an intelligent time frame, barring the unforeseen and/or poor assumptions (someone who is thought to be all in favor of the coaching is actually adamantly against it).

Retainer

A retainer in this context is not a legal-type retainer, which is merely a deposit against hourly billing deductions. (Never allow an attorney to tell you how to establish fees or conduct your marketing!)

Retainers are for access to your smarts. Their value is based on

- Who has access (one person, more than one person, client and buyer, and so on)
- Degree of access (during business hours, after hours, based on what time zones)
- Scope of access (phone, e-mail, personal meetings)

Retainers differ from the parasitic coach I mentioned because they are intended to serve as access to your intelligence on an "as needed" basis, and are reactive. This is where coaching does approach mentoring (see our definitions in Chapter 1). The proactive coaching relationship evolves into a reactive one, with the coach becoming a mentor to be accessed as needed.

It is ideal to establish these relationships with top, high-performing people who evolve rapidly, take on new challenges, and prefer to work only when needed with someone with whom they already have a trusting relationship.

Retainers generally run for a minimum of three months postcoaching, but may run for a year or more. Many of my retainer clients call only once a month or less, or send me an occasional e-mail. For them, the value is in knowing that I'm there and that I'm highly responsive when they need me. A retainer relationship is totally about quality and not quantity. (Many coaches feel guilty when their retainer clients haven't called, suffering because they feel they haven't justified their existence, which is a major self-esteem issue—for the coach, not the client.)

It's natural to move from a coaching project into a retainer relationship, particularly with senior people and those on "fast tracks." You can establish these time frames with the buyer, so that there is never a misunderstanding, and time doesn't "roll over." Months simply elapse.

Finally, determine time frames using my "80 percent ready, move" rule, which you can see in Figure 3-2. Every coaching and consulting project that I've ever undertaken has required midcourse correction and real-time fine-tuning. Don't wait for things to be perfect, either for yourself or for your client. The final 10 percent of preparation, seeking "perfection," will require 80 percent of your time and labor! And that final 20 percent is seldom, if ever, appreciated.

That is, the attempts to "perfect" the performance, actions, behavior, and results usually result in indiscernible dif-

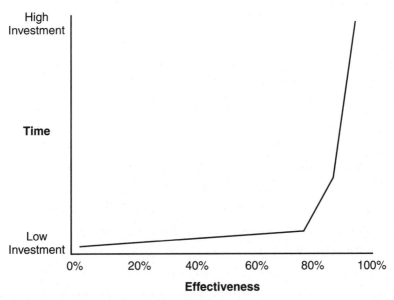

Figure 3-2   The 80 Percent Ready, Move Rule

ferences from merely improving them significantly. If you seek perfection, you'll overdeliver every time. That will decrease your wealth—your discretionary time—and won't help to improve the client's condition.

SELECTING EFFECTIVE METHODOLOGIES

There are a LOT of alternative tools for coaching well. You should have a large toolkit to avoid Maslow's admonition that if you have only a hammer, you tend to see every problem as a nail. Ideally, you should provide your buyer with several implementation options in the proposal, the least of which will meet the objectives (otherwise it's unethical to suggest it), with the others providing even more value because of additional features. I favor "escalating" these options, from basic to most sophisticated.

Simplistic example: Gain employee feedback on bonus plan changes.

Option 1: Survey people to get responses. Advantages include wide sweep, rapid use with technology, and guaranteed confidentiality. Disadvantages include the fact that most respondents are self-selecting, with no chance for follow-up.

Option 2: Survey with individual interviews. Advantages include follow-up questions and the ability to randomly select a cross section of diverse employees. Disadvantages include potential for less confidentiality and personal agendas being expressed.

Option 3: Survey, interviews, and focus groups. Advantages include the self-sanctioning aspect of groups, follow-up questions, and varied debate. Disadvantages include the lowest level of confidentiality and fear of others' perceptions of comments.

Option 1 would do the job, but option 3 provides a much more varied approach, heightening the advantages while compensating for the disadvantages, and if the patterns derived are consistent across all three techniques, then that is very reliable feedback.

Now, let's get back to coaching. Here are the basic tools in your kit:

1. *Shadowing.* You follow your client, listening and observing diverse situations, from presentations to evaluations and from making decisions to receiving client communications.

2. *360-degree assessments.* You interview the client's peers, subordinates, superiors, and/or clients to learn

patterns of behavior and obtain evidence of his
success or lack of success.

3. *Interview the client.* You interview the client in depth
at various times (at the outset, after key events, after
setbacks, and so forth) so that you can learn the
factors that influenced—rightly or wrongly—her
consequent behavior.

4. *Instruments.* There is a wide variety of instruments
available to measure behavioral styles, truth, integrity,
stress, aptitudes, and so forth.[4]

5. *Interviewing others.* This can include the cohort in the
360-degree assessment, but without a formalized set
of questions, and it can also include professional
associates, vendors, and relevant others.

6. *In-basket exercises.* These put the client in a situation
that replicates what he might be asked to handle in a
day or a week, and you observe what he does and
how he does it.

7. *Simulations and games.* These place the client—often
with others—in dynamic simulations of key job issues
that change frequently as the other participants make
decisions and take action.

8. *Case studies.* These are relevant situations (often real,
historical ones) that place the client in a current,
future, or other relevant position to assess how she
reacts when compared to the "real" resolution.

---

[4] Careful. Some of these are validated; some are like horoscopes.
Many of them need to be administered by a licensed psychologist. You're
better off allying yourself with someone who is duly licensed when you
need this rather than buying something "off the shelf" that has little true
value. You have to be a semiotician to understand half of the abstruse
labels that are applied. Remember, you're dealing with careers here.

9. *Assessment centers.* These can be run by the client or by an outside firm and incorporate a combination of these other tools to establish an evaluation in a relatively concise time frame.

10. *Observe and respond.* You view a particular event—for example, a presentation to the board or the termination of an employee—and then immediately debrief with the client.

11. *Rehearsals.* You simulate an approaching event so that the client can practice in safe conditions, not unlike a "mock jury" in the legal profession.

12. *Pre- and postassessments.* Using a number of these other options, you formally establish a beginning "baseline" for the client, perhaps an "average" for those in similar positions, a desired level of achievement, and then an actual level of performance at periodic intervals.

The selection of effective methodologies depends on several factors. Normally, you would combine various permutations of the dozen just listed into three or four "packages," which would be the options in your proposal.

Stop It! Don't throw everything but the kitchen sink into a single "take it or leave it" offering. If you give options, you place the client in the position not of "Should I do it?" but rather "HOW should I do it?"

ALAN'S FACTORS FOR CHOOSING COACHING METHODOLOGIES

- *Escalating value.* Create "packages" that represent increased value, above and beyond merely meeting the objectives. For example, the most basic option would probably always include choice 1 in the preceding list, but only the most valuable (and most expensive) option would include choice 9).

- *The nonclient buyer.* If the buyer is someone other than the client, then he or she will have some vested interest in issues such as investment, timing, disruption to the operation, confidentiality, and so forth.

- *Environment.* In some cases, it's easy to run focus groups or talk to clients, and in others it's nearly impossible to do this for physical or cultural reasons.

- *Speed.* The client may have a legitimate need for urgency of resolution, rendering some of these choices inappropriate.

- *Personal preference.* Clients learn best and accept feedback best in various ways. You need to adjust your options for maximum impact and commitment.

- *Personalization.* The higher the client's level, the more personalized coaching must be. Standardized tests make less sense than customized questions and observations.

- *Access.* Will you be able to attend board meetings, or does your client travel 85 percent of the time? What's reasonable in terms of legitimate access?

- *Your skills.* We're not all adept at professionally applying every tool. Try to ensure that you work at your most effective pace while gradually learning additional methodologies. But don't use your client as a lab rat!

MAKING THE BUYER (AND THE CLIENT) RESPONSIBLE

Coaches are not people who "do" something to others, contrary to some of the crazy methodology you hear out there. Helping someone tread on hot coals or rappel down a mountain is not coaching; it's guidance through various experiences, no different from someone taking you through the Sistine Chapel. You don't ask the cicerone about the ceiling by yelling, "Hey, coach!"

Coaching is about partnering with the buyer and the client. When the buyer is not your client, then your responsibilities would include

- Adhering to your fee payment and expense reimbursement schedules
- Accessibility in person and by other avenues as required
- Reinforcement and support for the client
- Observance of confidentiality
- Nonintervention and noninterference
- Tough decisions if the client isn't responding well
- References, referrals, and/or testimonials following a successful project
- Provision of relevant documentation and histories
- Maintaining promises made to the client

- Adherence to your disengagement schedule
- Access to others as needed, including the client
- Administrative and scheduling support
- Coordination of teams being coached
- Toleration of minor disruptions
- Prompt responses and deadlines met

If the buyer is also the client, then the list should be modified to include the following:

- Separation between having hired you and commitment to be helped
- Personal accountability for implementation of agreed-upon behaviors/actions
- Avoidance of threats or recrimination in the face of adverse feedback
- Priority time
- Participation in any group activities required

The buyer's responsibility begins with the proposal stage. He or she agrees to the developmental objectives, metrics of success, and value to the individual and the organization—conceptual agreement. It continues with the key introductions and provision of materials, as relevant. It can be measured in terms of promptness of responses, meeting deadlines, and fulfilling requests. You want a votary, not a violator.

You can begin to learn whether this accountability will be accepted as early as your initial marketing meetings. If you're kept waiting, appointments are canceled, calls and e-mails are unreturned, and promises are broken, you can bet that such behavior will be consistent.

> *Stop It! Don't assume that lousy prospects will make good clients. Rude and unprofessional prospective buyers turn into overbearing tyrants as clients. You don't need this kind of business, because you won't be successful in that environment.*

We've covered rules of engagement, and it's useful to present these prior to any proposal's being proffered.

One of the greatest traps you can fall victim to in terms of poor accountability is allowing the buyer to present you with an arbitrary alternative, thus becoming the consultant, and asking you merely to fulfill it as a "pair of hands."

You'll hear things like this:

- We need someone to work with him for a month.
- We'd like a day a week to shore up her presentation skills.
- The team is spinning its wheels—the members need a retreat.
- We must get his commitment to better language.

You'll also hear assumptions based on no evidence, wrong evidence, flimsy evidence, or misinterpreted evidence:

- He's not a team player.
- She has no loyalty.
- He can't be assertive enough to manage others.
- She gets flustered in crisis situations.
- The subordinates don't like her.
- The subordinates like him too much.

In the first list, there are arbitrary solutions to the presumed issue: a retreat, a time frame, a skill that needs developing. In the second, there are all kinds of emotional and subjective judgments made that suggest more about the observer's behavior than about the subject's.

Once you begin with a "psychological" premise, emotional barriers will drop like the shields on the *Starship Enterprise*, and nothing is going to penetrate short of a Klingon 3.7 space torpedo. Telling someone that he or she is "not a team player" is not exactly an invitation to honest commentary.

However, observing the real evidence—that the person is 20 minutes late to every Friday morning meeting—may get an objective, nonemotional response: "I have to take my son to child care on Fridays, and they've closed off the exit ramp on the Interstate."

Part of accountability is ensuring that the buyer does not provide an arbitrary alternative, a pet theory, a preformed solution, or an emotional gallimaufry. There has to be agreement to view the existing behavior dispassionately based on what's evidentiary, and to proceed from there without assuming a cause.

Your objective is to help the buyer realize that you're on the buyer's side, and you're both on the client's side, and that it's up to your collaboration and cooperation to deliver the goods.

DELIVERING THE GOODS

HEY, I'M ON YOUR SIDE

HOW TO PROVIDE EFFECTIVE FEEDBACK

Feedback is the catalyst for personal improvement in a coaching environment. We've discussed some criteria earlier. But here, let's use my TESTING acronym:

- Timely
- Exact and specific
- Supported by evidence
- Testing understanding
- Improvement-oriented
- Nailed and accurate
- Gain possible

Timely

You can't save feedback in your cheeks like a chipmunk. "I recall several weeks ago that you didn't respond well to questions in the meeting, and I've been meaning to mention this," is not helpful feedback. Try to communicate at the time of the behavior (or at least the report by the client) about what should be done as a result.

Exact and Specific

The best and most useful feedback is detailed. That includes positive feedback. It's not much good to say, "Nice job," if the recipient of the good news isn't sure how to replicate the performance. The entire point of feedback is improvement, which entails the ability to correct weaknesses and repeat and improve on strengths.

All of us go much farther in improving on strengths than we do in correcting weaknesses. Coaching can be remedial, but it should more often be uplifting and advanced.

Instead of, "You could have handled the questions better," try this: "You need three steps—repeat the question, respond to it, and review with the questioner whether the question was satisfactorily answered. Look at the sequence as three 'Rs.' You never repeated the question, and one problem was that the audience didn't always hear it, and so couldn't appreciate your response."

Do you see the difference? A random observer could have made the first comment. Only a professional, sophisticated coach could have made the second (whether that person calls himself or herself a coach or not!).

Supported by Evidence

Conjecture doesn't make for good coaching. "It looked like people were really interested" doesn't compare to "The written feedback showed a high level of understanding of your points, with 90 percent claiming that they could use them immediately." "You weren't dressed very appropriately" pales next to "Everyone else had on professional business attire, and you were wearing jeans and sneakers. You weren't dressed as a peer of the group."

Testing Understanding

This is probably *the* most underused and misunderstood aspect of coaching feedback. The information you provide must be demonstrated to be helpful and useful, not simply something aleatory and circumstantial.

Consequently, you test with your client to see if the feedback is understood, is accepted, and will be applied. The kinds of questions to ask include

- How will you use this technique in your next presentation?
- What is the next opportunity you will have to perform this type of evaluation using this new factor?
- At what meetings or events will you be able to try out this approach?
- How will you know from others that the technique was received well and enabled you to do what you had intended?

Testing understanding is your guarantee that your pace is good, you can move on, lessons have been mastered, a foundation is being built, you have commitment and not merely compliance, you're using the right examples, and so forth. No feedback session is complete without your testing your client's understanding of the changes required or reinforcement needed, and where and how they will be applied.

This "milepost" for you and the client will set you apart from the average coach, who, no matter how good his or her intentions, doesn't focus on how well the feedback is being received, embraced, and employed.

Improvement-Oriented

All feedback is directed toward improvement, whether it's "positive" or "negative." In that context, all feedback may be construed as positive, if that's helpful. However, the pragmatic fact is that you must usually deliver both good news and bad news.

Don't worry about "starting with good news and then going to bad," which evokes the Pavlovian response that when good feedback is provided, the client doesn't listen, since the conditioning is that a good whack is going to follow. (People are just as smart as dogs in most cases.)

If you have a trusting relationship with your client, then the debriefings—scheduled and unscheduled—should contain whatever mix makes sense in light of the client's recent behavior and evidence. Don't forget that all feedback must be timely, so simply focus on what's transpired lately.

Nailed and Accurate

This sounds like an obviousity, but I hear coaches say, "I could be wrong, but it seemed that you ran about 10 minutes over schedule." Did I or didn't I?! One minute doesn't matter; 10 minutes probably does. Which is it?

Gain Possible

Your focus must be on correctable issues. Don't forget that skills are taught and behavior is modified. Robert Mager's dictum: "Could the person do it if his or her life depended on it?" is apt.

- If not, then there is a skill problem.
- If so, then there is an attitude problem.

Reflect on our earlier discussion of beliefs formulating attitudes that are manifested in behavior. Noncorrectable issues include

- Physical characteristics (e.g., being short or bald)
- Deep-seated beliefs (e.g., "I refuse to work with women")
- Profound lack of background (e.g., can't speak or learn the language)
- Disease and illness (e.g., you can't "coach" someone out of depression)
- Personality disorders (e.g., severe bullying or passive-aggressive actions)

Some noncorrectable issues can be readily tolerated, such as height or disability, but some cannot for some jobs, such as poor reflexes for a pilot.

> *Stop It! Coaching is a profession and a business, not a popularity contest or a "safe haven." While your language should be objective and empathetic, it should not be sympathetic and disingenuous. A coach is part baseball umpire. Call the pitches and the swings as you see them, and then work on how the batter can hit the next one better.*

HOW TO VALIDATE YOUR ASSUMPTIONS AND INFORMATION

There are two sources of assumptions, presumptions, and outright guesses:

1. The client provides them for you, often with great dignity and officialdom (reports, PowerPoint) that imply gravitas and verification, but are really only the result of the client's having expectable prejudices and unsupported beliefs about a business in which the client is immersed most hours of the day.

2. You provide them from your subconscious beliefs, based on past experiences, that what was true in one place will be true in another, or that the client is somehow damaged and at fault—this from someone who is immersed in his or her own profession without much daily challenge.

In other words, both you and the client can have your nose plastered too firmly against the window. Invalidated assumptions and unverified conclusions are the basilisks of coaching. They are hoary monsters that can create havoc with your project from the outset, causing fear and loathing.

If you think that I'm damaged and manifest that belief, then I'm going to react rather coolly to your suggestions. If you walk in expecting one condition and find a completely different one, then you're going to be very wary about everything else you've been told.

Here are some telltale signs of unsupported conclusions from the client:

- Our experience has been . . . (Yes, but is the condition the same now?)
- Whenever this happens, that also happens . . . (Right, but correlation is not synonymous with causation.)
- We believe that . . . (Of course, but a lot of people believe in the Loch Ness monster, also.)
- The consensus is . . . (Very good; of course, a camel is a consensus horse.)
- We recommend that . . . (Understandable, but you've suddenly become the coach in that case, and what good would I be?)
- We know that he is the one at fault . . . (Correct, and the stock market fluctuates daily, but the useful information would be "Why?")
- The last time this occurred . . . (. . . you obviously did not fix it.)

Here are the deadly demons that can color and taint your own objectivity:

- You immediately lapse into a methodology or set of responses based on past cases like the one presented.
- You begin to assume who's "at fault," and look for blame rather than cause.
- You take sides (for management, against management, for sales, against R&D).
- You ignore cognitive dissonance. You believe what you're told despite observing something else. (She is very patient listening to employees and granting exceptions to policy where needed, but others call her a tyrant and selfish.)
- You focus on the effects and not the cause.

This last point is very important, so here's a brief test. In the following scenario, about whom are you concerned?

Three employees approach their supervisor's manager and complain that the supervisor is unfair, hasn't lived up to promises of compensatory time or provided new equipment that is still sitting in storage. The manager has decided to ask for your help and not try to intervene himself, since he doesn't want to undercut the supervisor by dealing further with the three employees. He tells you that the supervisor has just returned from a two-week illness. This is the first time he's heard this complaint, and when he asks her how things are, she says, "Fine."

Whom are you concerned about?

I'm concerned about the employees, because they shouldn't be complaining, but they are. I don't know why; I simply know the secondhand version of what they're claiming. That's where I'm going to start. The manager probably should have discussed this with the supervisor, but that's not the priority concern. And I know nothing at all about the supervisor, other than that this is the first time this has occurred.

> *Stop It! Use what you can see, hear, and verify, not rumor, innuendo, or guesses. Remember that acting on the basis of poor evidence is as common in the executive suite as on the plant floor. They're just playing with more money.*

Coaching is a process, not an event, and it has to be built on a firm foundation. Otherwise, you may develop elaborate and breathtaking solutions to problems that don't exist, and make highly sophisticated decisions about alternatives that aren't relevant!

Here are some techniques to validate assumptions and "information" that you're given.

ALAN'S TECHNIQUES TO VERIFY VARIOUS VERSIONS

1. *Adopt a healthy dose of skepticism.* Think like a police detective or an investigative reporter. "Just the facts," as Jack Webb used to say on the old *Dragnet* series. Just because the client tells you something doesn't mean that it's empirically true, and just because the client is paying you doesn't mean the client is omniscient. Most clients will not lie maliciously, but they will lie unintentionally.

2. *Observe and find evidence.* Behavior—over the longer term, not a single instance—seldom lies. Determine whether what you're told is borne out in the real world.

3. *Look for patterns.* Once is an accident, twice is a coincidence, and three times is probably a pattern. If one person makes a comment, it may be just a personal perspective. If eight people make the same comment (e.g., "He is never prepared to lead the meeting and never follows the agenda"), then the observation is probably accurate.

4. *Ask for examples.* Instantiate the feedback; move it from the conceptual to the tangible. "She is certainly not a team player." "Really? What evidence or behavior can you cite to support that conclusion?"

5. *Go to the source.* If someone's name is constantly mentioned as the "problem" or the "sticking point," go talk to her. She may be paid by someone to be that obstacle, as in lawyer, or auditor, or quality control specialist.

6. *Simulate the conditions.* If someone is supposedly a poor listener and cuts off others' sentences in mid-

participle, engage him in conversation and see if the critique is borne out in real time.

The purpose of coaching is to bring your client from the current state to a preferred future state. You must make sure that the future state is attainable, and the expectations concerning it accurate. But prior to that, you must determine whether the current state is perceived realistically.

To cite the modern troubadour, Billy Joel, "The good old days weren't all that good and tomorrow ain't as bad as it seems."[1] Or vice versa.

DEALING WITH RESISTANCE AND WORSE

You don't always see what you're going to get. It's rare for disrespectful and unprofessional prospects to become good clients (run while you can), but it's less rare for seemingly willing and eager prospects to become lousy clients. Despite your best attempts and careful analysis, there is often a broken-down building behind the façade.

There are rational reasons for this:

- The client is not the buyer and wanted to please the buyer by showing his eagerness to improve.
- The coaching help is mandatory for everyone at a certain level, but this person doesn't see the need, other than to comply with organizational policy.
- The buyer is the client and actually acts differently in each role. She made an intellectual decision to hire

[1] From the album *An Innocent Man*, "Keeping the Faith" lyrics by Billy Joel (1998).

you, but then has an emotional reaction to actually using your help and advice.

- The expectation was incorrect. This may be the buyer's fault or yours or both of yours. What was somehow expected (e.g., an occasional pleasant discussion) was not borne out by your methodology (e.g., candid, direct assessments).

- Self-image is not consistent with reality, and the client expected vastly more positive feedback and felt that he was far better at the issues than your observations and feedback reflect.

- For some reason, you are not seen either as a peer or as a credible expert.

- Organizational priorities abruptly shift.

- Personal matters change and intervene.

- You do a poor job and it's apparent, or you violate your agreements (e.g., break confidentiality).

- Others are giving the client feedback that doesn't agree with yours.

That's quite a list! And I've seen all of it happen, sometimes with several of these issues arising in a single client!

The result of this is resistance, compliance rather than commitment, failure to use your advice, undermining of your work, and so on. In my experience, I've seen more attempts to undermine coaches than consultants (or to undermine the coaching aspects of consulting assignments) because the nature of the work is so very personal to the client. The private meetings of the client with the buyer, the rumors that circulate, the team that becomes hard to assemble—these are all indications that someone is trying to throw you down the stairs and out the door.

Fortunately, we know all this. So here is how you deal with these dynamics, which will inevitably arise during your career, so don't fear.

Preventive Measures

The best thing to do is to head this stampede off at the pass, as the old Western movies advised. If you prevent the likely causes, then the problem won't develop, so this is by far the most efficacious kind of action and should be a routine aspect of all your coaching work.

First, test for understanding with the buyer and the client. Never, ever, accept a coaching assignment without meeting the client. The buyer alone, without the client, is insufficient, and HR is always irrelevant. Make sure that both the buyer and the client understand how you will work, the accountabilities of all parties, the methods and nature of the communications, the limits of confidentiality, and what should occur if someone is unhappy. That's right, set up the procedures for grievances at the outset.

We've already discussed alternative methodologies, so you should explain the nature, demands, and consequences of those varying techniques (or at least the ones that you're fairly certain will apply with this client). Establish the relationships among the buyer, the client, and yourself or the team, the buyer, and yourself.

Ask the client to formally acknowledge these conditions and approaches. Include them as an appendix to the proposal. If the buyer signs the proposal and is not the client, have the client sign the addendum personally.

Prepare your buyer for the rumors and complaints that often accompany coaching (especially team coaching, where individual performance isn't consistent). Make a deal: "If you don't believe everything you hear about me, I won't believe everything I hear about you."

Finally, do a great job. Prepare carefully. Make no offhand comments, and don't be sarcastic. The one guarantee about secrets in organizational life is that there ARE no secrets.

Contingent Measures

Sometimes preventive actions fail to stop the cause. You may have missed a cause, or the preventive action may have been ignored or ineffective. Telling someone, for instance, that she shouldn't listen to inexperienced people trying to give her feedback doesn't ensure that the advice will be heeded. And you really can't establish preventive actions with 100 percent coverage—shifting business and personal priorities are a fact of life.

So if a problem occurs, and the client is resistant, resentful, or reproaching, follow these guidelines:

1. *Acknowledge the disagreement.* Don't assess blame or culpability; merely state, "Carol, I think we disagree about your performance with the team at that client meeting, so why don't we talk about it factually and decide what the actual performance was?"

2. *Use evidence.* Don't tell someone that his ego is too involved. You may indeed find yourself coaching flâneurs and poseurs at times, but even with them, attacking them emotionally doesn't work. Instead, say: "You're telling me that your evaluation session went well, yet your subordinate didn't say more than 10 words and slammed the door. That's what I saw. What did you see that led you to think otherwise?"

3. *Ask what would make the client happy.* This will usually be far less than you might have alternatively offered.

For example, your client may say, "I need feedback closer to my actual performance, and in person. The next morning by e-mail doesn't work for me. I'd like you to stay longer and provide it immediately, even if your notes are incomplete."

4. *Never take abuse.* Language should always be professional. Deadlines should be met. Tackle this head-on, and threaten to stop work immediately and report the behavior (even if your client and buyer are the same) if it doesn't change immediately.

5. *Consider delaying or even terminating the relationship.* If business priorities are severe and real, allow the project to go into hiatus (assuming that you can't make the case that the buyer needs you more than ever amidst the change). If personal issues are severe, you may want to suggest that the project be ended.[2]

> *Stop It! You're not coaching to be loved. You can get a dog for that. Don't subvert your own effectiveness by seeking strokes for yourself, or refrain from pointing out problems and lack of commitment just because it may make you temporarily unpopular. You can't pay the mortgage with popularity.*

Figure 4-1 is a guide to help you understand the power of your actions to prevent and deal with resistance and other problems that emerge in coaching.

---

[2] Which is why you should always be paid in advance, or at least near the beginning of the project. See the chapter on fees.

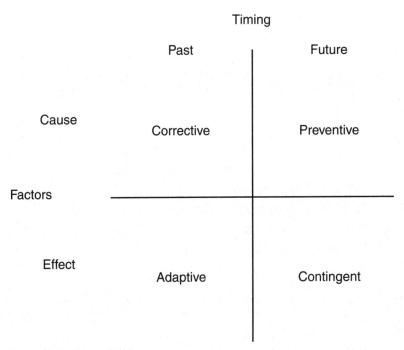

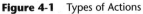

Figure 4-1   Types of Actions

Corrective action is aimed at an event that has already occurred, and for which you want to remove the cause and eliminate it entirely.

Example: The client complains that the buyer is asking for reports of progress that are uncalled for and uncomfortable. You ask the buyer to review your rules of engagement and agreements, and ask that such requests stop. The cause of the problem is removed.

Adaptive action is intended to reduce the effects of problems that arise, regardless of the cause.

Example: The client is resisting meeting with you because there is no real privacy in the business and he feels uncomfortable about being seen working with you. Adaptive action: meet off-site. The lack of privacy remains, but it's no longer causing the problem.

Preventive action is created to avoid and eliminate causes of future problems.

Example: If confidentiality is a key issue, you apprise the client and the buyer that communications and feedback are only between you and the client unless the client decides otherwise, but that there can be no pressure from the buyer to make that happen.

Contingent action is created to deal with the effects of problems should they occur anyway (preventive action was not possible or failed).

Example: The client informs you of a loss of key personnel, leading to impossible demands on her time. You have established beforehand the agreement that the coaching can be placed on a 30-day "freeze" when emergencies occur, with the agreement that weekly phone calls will be used to keep momentum at a certain minimal level. The client and the buyer have both agreed to this ahead of time.

Resistance can occur. The key over the long term is to try to prevent it, but also to have mechanisms in place to cope with it effectively and mitigate it should it arise.

AVOIDING THE POLITICAL

The following case study leads us into a realm that is too often dismissed in the same vein as, "Watch out for the cafeteria meat loaf."

Political content in organizations varies from the watercooler to the boardroom. To a very real extent, it's impossible to eradicate. But it can interfere with your coaching, so it's best to be aware of what the dynamics are in any given client.

In Figure 4-2, I've made two simple conditions. An organization has only 100 percent of its resources and energies to spend. I have no idea what is meant when a manager says, "Let's

CASE STUDY: The Unchangeable

I was asked to coach an executive vice president called Ron. He was the son of the founder of the company, which had grown to a billion dollars and had been sold to a corporate giant. His father had long since retired, but the current president had promised that he would always look after Ron.

Ron was in his early forties, and he never failed to meet the sales goals for his unit. However, he was a ruthless, obscene, and tyrannical boss who regularly screamed at people in public, threw things, stomped out of meetings, ridiculed his peers—you get the idea. He had been through four coaches and had never changed a whit.

I had been consulting and coaching with the new parent organization for a decade. They asked me to meet with the division president and take on the "Ron issue." The president welcomed my help, urged me to change Ron's dysfunctional behaviors, and gave me carte blanche.

I observed all the horrible behavior I had been warned about. When I met with Ron, he immediately agreed with everything we discussed, promised to improve, welcomed my help—and didn't change a thing! This went on for two weeks.

I met with the president and told him that Ron wasn't about to change, and that the work he was doing was not so unique that someone else from this division or the parent couldn't handle it. The president told me of his commitment to protect Ron, and speculated that people would simply accept him as an idiosyncratic but successful executive.

He asked that I continue working with Ron, and I refused. I told him that he had, in fact, two options:

1. He could remove Ron from that position, either by moving him to a less public position or terminating him with proper severance.
2. I could go back to the parent—and my buyer—and tell it to do the same thing.

The president was aghast at those prospects, but then I sealed the deal. "You know, people in your division assume that you are as vicious and vindictive as Ron."

(continued on next page)

CASE STUDY: **The Unchangeable** *(continued)*

"Impossible!" he shouted. "I'm interacting with everyone daily, listening, supporting."

"Yes, but you're also supporting Ron's behavior through your passivity. People know he couldn't act that way without your implicit or explicit approval, and so do your superiors at the parent."

That was it; Ron was gone. It took a month, but he departed.

Lessons:
- Some people can't or won't change, and you are a coach, not a savior.
- Pathologically dysfunctional behavior requires therapy, not coaching.
- Find the self-interest of the buyer to gain support.
- Always consider the greater good.

---

give it 110 percent!" There is a finite amount of energy, and the question is simple: is it directed toward internal, political issues, or toward external, client issues?

In the best companies that I've worked with (or observed), the ratio is about 10/90. That is, 10 percent of the energy is

Where Is the Energy Going?

100% of Organization Energies

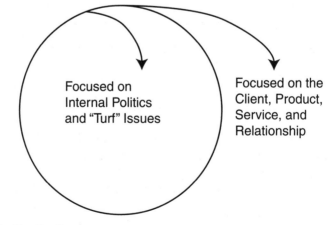

Focused on Internal Politics and "Turf" Issues

Focused on the Client, Product, Service, and Relationship

Figure 4-2   Directing Energy

abraded away internally, but 90 percent of it is directed toward sales, service, retention, market share, and so forth.

But in the worst, the energies are overwhelmingly invested in questions and issues such as

- Why does she have that office and I have this smaller one?
- Why is he getting that assignment and not me?
- Have you heard that the compensation plan will change next year?
- I think we can leave earlier on Fridays without being noticed.
- Have you heard of job openings down the street?

You can never eradicate the office grapevine, but you can create an environment in which most of the energies most of the time are directed toward and supportive of the organization's strategic goals and tactical requirements.

How do you know if there is a strong political content? That is, how can you tell what percentage of energies are inside my circle?

ALAN'S POLITICAL ANALYSIS TECHNIQUES

- Does your buyer and/or client talk in terms of "winning" or of "beating" internal colleagues?
- Is most of the talk about colleagues and not clients?
- Is the coaching viewed as necessary to "please" someone internally, instead of as an important performance improvement requirement?

- Are there people you are told to avoid or to make sure you talk to, not necessarily for the value of their inputs, but because "they must be included and feel as if they've been consulted"?
- Are there certain topics or subjects that you're told can't be discussed?
- Does the client continually talk about others and their effects on his performance, rather than about his own ability to improve?
- Is the client more concerned about what will make the buyer happy than about what will help her improve her ability to do the job?
- Are you prohibited from speaking to certain peers, or clients, or even subordinates?

It's natural to sign nondisclosure forms and confidentiality agreements with any client. But it's not natural or unavoidable to be embroiled in political wars.

> *Stop It! There's nothing wrong with telling your client, "Look, you keep talking about 'conditions' and about what 'they' might do. Why don't we focus on your behavior and what you have to do to maximize your success and your organization's success?"*

If you are facing an overtly political climate, it doesn't mean that you have to stop working or can't be effective. But it does mean that you have to take certain precautions.

First, use the previous criteria to determine the extent of the political influence. My rule of thumb is that anything over 25/75 is an issue. In other words, if more than a quarter of the discussion, focus, orientation, behavior, and so on is oriented toward internal concerns, then I judge that to be a significant political climate.[3] I have seen and worked in organizations with ratios as high as 75/25. The key is to understand that, and act accordingly.

Second, "acting accordingly" starts with never taking sides. I don't care who hired you or who the client is. You must focus on the client's improvement as manifested in better job performance, not better swordsmanship with internal "competitors." Embrace sources of input wherever you normally would, without restriction. Don't engage in name-calling or deny respect to other areas.

Third, stop those with you from engaging in political behavior in your presence, or you're passively supporting it (see my case study about Ron). If the client or buyer (or anyone else present, such as a team member) says, "We're going to have a tough time improving customer relations as long as the call center employs people who can't think without a script," you need to respond, "Let's not worry about people we don't control, but let's try to influence whomever we can through the new actions we're talking about."

Fourth, don't become a backstage gossip yourself. Tell your buyer and/or client what they need to hear given your charter and responsibilities, but there is no need to tell them that you think you saw a private meeting with the divisional vice president and two people from another department who were deemed to be in competition. That's not helpful. Don't try to win "points" through some kind of political collaboration.

---

[3] Note: Focusing on internal matters such as better use of technology and improved environments for working is not political. I'm strictly talking about interpersonal and interdepartmental resentments, lobbying, favoritism, and so on.

Fifth, hedge your bets and be professional with and respectful to everyone. You never know where your repeat business might come from. Never reveal progress or results to anyone who shouldn't be privy to such things, but do be cordial, explain your processes, and offer informal assistance if it's not laborious and will ingratiate you with potential future clients.

All organizations have a political context. That's normal and natural. They are nonetheless valid and productive businesses that can profit from your help with their key personnel. It's your job to remain professional and independent as you engage in that process.

You're a coach, not a political collaborator.

Let's turn now to how to be great at the art and science of coaching.

METHODOLOGIES, TECHNOLOGIES, AND ANALOGIES

THE MILLION DOLLAR COACHING TOOLKIT

INTERPERSONAL TECHNIQUES

Let's delve further into the kinds of alternatives that exist within the methodologies you choose. These are not meant to be all-inclusive, but to represent a cross section of types of pragmatic help that don't demand special degrees or certifications and that you can create and customize for clients, thereby increasing your value.

We'll begin with a category that I call "interpersonal techniques," meaning that you are physically interacting with your client.

Observation and Feedback

Watching someone is very instructive, assuming that you know what you're looking for! In observation, you're not so much looking for the gestalt of a person's day, but rather for those instances that relate to the developmental objectives that you've established.

For example, if the developmental objective is to better develop subordinates, you'd want to observe

- *Requests from subordinates for help.* Does your client provide techniques and ideas for solving their problems, or does he solve the problems for them?
- *Choices about investment in development.* Does your client actively elicit perceived needs from her subordinates, or does she simply assign them training (or allow HR to do so)?
- *Reactions to complaints about subordinates.* Does the client castigate the person involved, or instead ask what the person intends to do to placate whoever has complained?

The key to observations, which I also called "shadowing" earlier, is to arrange the time so that you're likely to see occasions and examples of the behavior in question.

Assessment

In these instances, you are observing a specific event or dynamic. You may be watching a presentation to management, or a subordinate evaluation session, or outward-bound phone calls to clients. You are assessing the specific situations that are causing a problem or for which further growth is desired.

This is similar to observation and feedback, but it differs in that it can be highly localized, specified, and arranged.

Rehearsals and Role-Plays

In these cases, both you and the client are practicing. He or she may be giving a presentation intended for an employee meeting, or pretending to be at a sales call, or handling a complaint.

These role-plays can be based on actual events that are approaching or be created examples that are based on likely or past scenarios. The advantage of role-plays is that they can be repeated over a very brief time span, aren't dependent on certain events transpiring, and allow for you and the client to switch roles as appropriate.

Stop It! Don't wait for the "perfect moment" to observe and interact with your client. Observe frequently enough so that certain events are more likely to occur, and recreate those that are readily replicable.

360-Degree Assessments

I've included these here, rather than in "Instrumented Techniques," because I think you should create them and not rely on off-the-shelf or electronic versions.

A 360-degree assessment is simply a series of interviews with the client's normal contacts, as agreed upon by the client and you (and the buyer, if necessary). They typically include a combination of peers, subordinates, superiors, clients, suppliers, and any other normal relationships at work.

Once again, to develop an effective 360-degree assessment, you must know what the desired information is. For example, if you're trying to determine how the client sets priorities, then your questions should be consistent, but not obvious. Instead of asking, "How does he set priorities?" you'd want to ask questions such as, "How does he choose what to do himself and what to delegate?" or "Are deadlines ever missed, and why or why not?"

Ideally, you should

- Develop your list of interviewees.
- Schedule interviews, explaining their nature:
  - The person and the issues
  - Total confidentiality
  - Length
- Generally take about 20 to 40 minutes, depending upon how loquacious the interviewee is.
- Take notes carefully, and read them back to check their accuracy at the conclusion.
- Have six to eight questions, and add follow-up questions as you hear the responses.
- As early patterns emerge, add them as questions for subsequent interviews.
- Hide anything that may betray confidentiality.[1]
- Report back to the client when you have completed the assessment and have a pattern of results—never use "one-off" or single opinions in your feedback.

When you are coaching a team, you can combine questions about all the members in each interview, and you can choose to report back individually or to the team as a group. (I recommend that you do both, saving more sensitive individual feedback for private meetings.)

Serendipity

One of the benefits of private, interpersonal coaching is that things happen in real time. You may observe things that the

---

[1] If the sole person in the department who travels reports that travel expenses are not approved quickly enough, you'll have to deal with this in another manner.

client hasn't reported not because he is trying to conceal them, but because they aren't apparent to him—the client has a blind spot. They may or may not be within the developmental objectives, but they don't constitute "scope creep"—that is, it's safe and a good idea to mention the fact that the client forgets to say "thank you" or parks in the wrong parking spot.

If you're focused on the developmental objectives to begin with, you'll avoid a farrago of feedback, and you'll be entitled to add some things that you feel it is in the best interests of your client to include.

We all want to be told that we tend to get lettuce stuck in our teeth, so we might want to avoid the Caesar salad when we are dining with the boss in the executive dining room. And it's also helpful to know when you're calling someone by the wrong name consistently!

REMOTE TECHNIQUES

Because of both technology and our acceptance of its limitations, the opportunity to coach remotely is both acceptable and effective.

Some of this remote coaching may be interspersed with the interpersonal techniques discussed in the previous section: you follow up by phone, the client sends you an e-mail, and so on. But you can conduct entire coaching projects remotely these days, and they can be highly efficacious.

Thus, by "remote techniques," I mean approaches that can be used either in coordination with more personal avenues or completely by themselves. The latter has become much more common with the synergistic growth of globalized economies and advancing technology.

My key buyer at Hewlett-Packard had asked me to help with a brief coaching need, and we both agreed that it should take about a month and that the fee would be $50,000.

"When will you be here?" she asked. (The HP site was in Mountain View, California, and I live in Rhode Island.)

"I won't," I pointed out.

"You won't be here at ALL?"

"No."

"Why not?"

"Whom do you report to?"

"You know whom I report to: George in Brussels."

"And to whom does he report?"

"Carl in Hong Kong."

"Do you ever get together in person?"

"No."

"Well, I'm just trying to fit in." The project was completed remotely.

Here are the remote techniques that are available to you at this writing, but watch the appendix to this book on my site (noted in the Appendix) for updates:

- E-mail

  Advantages: "Time shifts" interactions well; can use attachments, including audio and video.

  Disadvantages: No inflections or intonations; can be hastily sent and can't be effectively recalled;[2] sometimes not secure and private.

- Phone

  Advantages: Voice tone can be used and heard; quick real-time interaction; useful for role-plays; can be spontaneous.

[2] Try placing outgoing e-mails in a draft or other folder and waiting an hour before sending anything that is emotionally charged or in response to sensitive issues.

Disadvantages: No nonverbal behavior; inappropriate when there are large time zone differences; tedious for lengthy conversations; can be interruptions. (Cell phones remain pretty horrible for this type of work, and I suggest a landline.)

- Skype® and related technologies

  Advantages: Combines phone with visual contact; very inexpensive; can be spontaneous.

  Disadvantages: Technology is erratic; time zone problems; limited to "talking heads."

- Virtual offices (video technology that places the other's environment adjacent to yours)

  Advantages: Highly realistic; virtual physical interactions.

  Disadvantages: Very expensive; requires special equipment; must be in designated places to utilize it.

Stop It! Don't "default" to personal or remote coaching. Find out what's in the best interests of the client and choose the most effective and practical means or combinations.

The ideal situations for pragmatic, important, and comprehensive coaching combine interpersonal and remote measures. The better the relationship, the better remote measures work, because the trust needed to overcome communications glitches and errors is present. There is seldom second-guessing about "What did she really mean by that?"

In an ideal world, my experience is that a major coaching project would include about 40 percent interpersonal work and 60 percent remote work. The more you shift from the latter to the former, the more you reduce labor intensity, but don't do that at the expense of your client's improvement velocity. When the client says, "Where have you been? I've needed you," that's a tocsin to warn you that what you considered adequate remote communication wasn't perceived that way by your client.

When does solely remote coaching work? Under the following conditions or combinations thereof.

ALAN'S REMOTE COACHING CRITERIA

- The issues are not comprehensive but focused; for example, the client requires help in writing briefer reports or dealing with organization, rather than better sales closing techniques with diverse clients.
- The circumstances make interpersonal coaching inappropriate and/or too expensive: distance, travel schedules, budgets, and so on.
- Your brand is so strong that people are willing to accept you on a remote basis, given the repute of your work and results.
- You are dealing with a market that has little money and only situational needs, such as small businesses, nonprofits, education, and so on.
- The client groups are accustomed to and prefer remote assistance, for example, sales forces, repair people, or the military.
- You do not want to travel if at all possible.
- You own or have access to technology that can maximize your remote effectiveness.
- Privacy is such a compelling issue that even off-site meetings can be too risky for the client.

We'll discuss in the fees chapter how to differentiate and charge for these various modalities. But for now, bear in mind that interpersonal coaching is usually best but may not always be possible, and that remote coaching has become quite common and is becoming more effective each day as technology continues to enable it.

INTERNET AND ELECTRONIC TECHNIQUES

Let's focus for a while on the Internet and its incredible capacity to provide amazing remote help or incredible distant harm. Increasingly, coaches are able to interact with clients near and far without the need for physical presence. How do you make the best of that and avoid the worst?

First, keep the following criteria and guidelines in mind.

A Portion of Your Communication Will Be Missing

There is no substance to the wild claims that more than half of our communications effectiveness comes from nonverbal behavior—words are the tools of the coaching profession—but it's undeniable that nonverbal behavior is the seasoning to the nutrition. Coaching by phone, e-mail, fax, and even using the video alternatives mentioned earlier, such as Skype, will never allow for the "body language" nuances that accentuate the language.

Consequently, you have to be extremely careful to test for understanding, and you have to be willing to listen very carefully. An on-site coach can have a lupine posture, waiting to pounce after observing certain behaviors. A remote coach must be more patient and softer on the approach.

When the client uses a behavior and you observe that behavior (especially repeatedly), you have unequivocal evidence for your feedback. But when the client merely explains what he or she perceives has occurred, you have the problem of many filters and agendas intervening.

Thus, ask questions such as

- What, specifically, did others say? Please be as precise as you can.
- What did you observe them to do? Describe their exact actions.
- Why have you reached this conclusion? What's your evidence?
- When and where did this occur? Under what conditions?

And ask testing questions such as

- How will you change your behavior in this situation next time?
- What will you say differently in the future?
- How will you avoid this situation next week?
- What will you use to "trigger" or remind yourself of new responses?

> *Stop It! Don't use identical behaviors in person and remotely. Adjust to compensate for the disadvantages of not being present and accentuate the advantages of being able to deal remotely.*

You Will Be Able to Interact More Frequently

"Real-time" coaching is augmented by the use of technology, since the client is able to contact you and (potentially) obtain feedback at critical junctures. (Whether you are dealing only remotely or in a combination with interpersonal presence, this is quite valuable.) I've been in the position of being able to help someone by texting or e-mailing back and forth on iPhones just prior to a key meeting or challenge of some sort. I've had people text me during meetings, although I discourage it for obvious reasons. You can't get much more "real time" than that![3]

You must be careful not to create a codependency. Coaching is about transferring skills and modifying behaviors. But a codependency is created when the client contacts you about virtually all important matters, including those that you have already discussed and resolved in the past, meaning that skills transfer hasn't taken place. In other words, you've become Google rather than a guide. (I don't have to learn to spell this word; I can always look it up electronically. I don't need to master creating a meeting agenda; I can always e-mail it to my coach for improvement.)

Keep remote sessions relatively brief. Create rules about expected response time from both of you. For example:

- Phone calls returned within three hours (assuming a common time zone).
- E-mail returned within a day.
- Texts returned within one hour.

[3] I wouldn't advise a client to consult with me during a meeting if I were sitting there, nor would I advise him or her to text me if I'm not there.

- Access is 9 to 5, local business hours.
- Scheduled calls once a week for 30 minutes, Friday mornings at 10.
- Notification of breaks in the routine (vacation, travel) one week ahead.
- Exceptions as requested, e.g., Sunday night prior to board meeting.

You get the idea. You can arrange for "remote rules of engagement" that create a personalized relationship even though you may not ever physically be present with your client.

You Will Have Limited Access to the Environment and Others

Perhaps the greatest drawback is that you're almost totally reliant on your client (and/or your buyer) to create a picture of the surroundings and of other parties, both of which strongly affect your client and your client's behavior. There are techniques to consider to mitigate this problem:

- Gain permission to talk to significant others, preferably by phone, but at least by e-mail. This may include peers, subordinates, customers, and so on. Have the buyer or client "personally" introduce you and your role to these others.
- Don't laugh: have the client send you photos or even videos of the environment and significant others. It helps tremendously if you have a mental picture of where your client is operating, and with current technology, that's an easy favor to grant. Include your client's work area.

- Diligently examine the client's organization's Web site, written materials, and collateral. Try to get a "flavor" of the culture.
- Test with your client any assumptions you have:
  - Was the meeting around a conference table or in an auditorium?
  - How are people dressed at these meetings?
  - Are people focused, or are they looking at their watches?
  - What time of day was it?

It actually helps to think a bit like a police detective. Get a view of the "scene" so that you can test your own conclusions and develop hypotheses.

Remote work through technology can be a boon if you maximize the advantages but are also astute enough to minimize the disadvantages. (We'll cover the differences in pricing later, when we talk about fees.)

Think of that e-mail you sent that, a nanosecond later, you wished you had never written. Think of the misimpressions you've had corrected once you arrived somewhere for which you had a vastly different picture in your mind. Think of the times you have misinterpreted, for better or worse, a technological communication from business associates.

You can't afford to allow these problems to arise when other people's careers and futures are on the line. You can't allow it technologically, nor with tests and assessments.

INSTRUMENTED TECHNIQUES

And now we move into dangerous waters, so please conform with the lifeboat drills.

There are tests, and then there are tests. They range from highly regarded, long-term psychological instruments to tarted-up horoscopes that are merely meant to provide coaches with additional streams of income. (There are also people who tell me that they are psychic or "intuitors" and who tell me highly insightful things that no one else would ever discern, such as that I enjoy using my pool or driving my Bentley.)

Historically, in validating tests, the American Psychological Association has used standards such as

- *Criterion validity.* How well do the test variables predict a described outcome?
- *Content validity.* How well does a measure represent the entire social construct, for example, are certain important dimensions present or ignored in the test?
- *Concurrent validity.* Do test results correlate with previously validated results? (In other words, would current excellent performers score highly on a test that purportedly measures that performance?)
- *Test-retest reliability.* Do test results remain basically constant for the same person taking the test under the same circumstances, or do results vary for no apparent reason?

I'll stop short of Psychology 101, but I'll point you toward the APA and suggest that test validation—not merely for the test generically, but for the test within various cultural contexts (organizations)—is an expensive, lengthy process. Longitudinal studies are designed to assess testing efficacy over various time periods.

Even highly regarded tests have strange origins. The famous Minnesota Multiphasic Personality Inventory was designed to see who was fit for combat during World War II, and its test basis was rural farmers. The Myers-Briggs Type Indicator (MBTI) was designed by a woman with no psychological background whatsoever.

Leaving all of that aside, let me make several key points:

1. Most traditional tests were designed to separate out dysfunctional and unhealthy behavior, not to discriminate and label various types of healthy behavior. Therefore, the stereotypical four-quadrant results (e.g., "Feeler," "Driver," "High I," "Red," "Earth") are rather arbitrary categories based on simplistic criteria.

2. Any label immediately creates a set of preconceptions on the part of the labeler. "What do you expect from an Analytic?" is not helpful in understanding or influencing the other person, but rather relegates him or her to a disparaging category. (And it's only an inch short of beliefs such as, "What do you expect of a woman in that position?")

3. Most "forced choice" tests have inherent flaws because they force a choice even when you may honestly find all options equally appealing or equally repellant. If there are enough such questions, the results are notoriously inaccurate.

4. Many tests have woeful biases in terms of gender, ethnicity, and culture.

5. Any test that costs you $12 so that you can sell it for $24 is exclusively designed to provide a revenue stream of sorts, not a comprehensive analysis.

6. Tests that don't require extensive personal study and performance standards for the user (usually including psychological training) are always suspect.

> *Stop It! You are not helping people by labeling*
> *them. That applies to Gen X, Boomers, the*
> *Greatest Generation, or Amiable Imploders. This*
> *may come as a surprise, but coaches had better*
> *appreciate that people are individuals, first and*
> *foremost.*

Tests and their "results" often serve as an emollient as well, rationalizing and soothing certain behaviors and results. They compare people to others or to arbitrary norms, ignoring the individual and his or her context. I once watched a client struggle with raising the "leadership quotients" of all the top people in a dozen categories. The conversations were exclusively about "going from 6.1 to 6.4," the minimum for an "acceptable response" in that category. It was lunacy. No one cared about actual behavior, only the decimal points in the testing results. I had to use dynamite to bring this to a halt.

If you choose to use tests, your best bet is to ally yourself with professionals in the psychological community who are duly licensed and trained (unless you are a clinician yourself). For example, in coaching an individual at a major newspaper who was having chronic problems in each job assigned him, I had suspicions that he was depressed. I sought permission to use a colleague who was a licensed therapist to test him, and, sure enough, that was the conclusion. It was a shock for him and his family, but they accepted the suggested course of treatment given the legitimacy of the evaluation.

And you can't coach someone out of depression.

Remember that you are not a therapist, and even if you have those credentials, you're not acting as one when you're in the role of a coach. Despite some people feeling that they have a "calling" to act in this capacity, coaching and therapy are two different undertakings. Once you start asking people what their mother did to cause their current behavior, you're walking on thin ice with a flamethrower turned on and pointed at your feet.

Can these abuses really happen? Well, while working in a major New York bank, I found a certified "analyst" from a testing company (he was "certified" by virtue of having gone through a few days of training) asking an executive vice president a set of questions from the testing instruments. But the vice president was responding as he thought his deceased mother would respond! Why? Because the two of them were trying to resolve "unresolved conflicts between him and his mother."

I turned them in. You might as well hold a séance.

My coaching advice to you:

- Don't use tests from the Internet or that you purchase inexpensively from "suppliers."
- Don't use tests for which you do not have extensive training in their administration, interpretation, and feedback.
- Do try to find legitimate sources that are available in alliance with qualified and professional administrators.
- Do use your judgment and observations, and merely note categories and labels suggested by an instrument.

At their best, tests are merely one source of feedback to augment many others that only you can create and apply. At their worst, they are self-fulfilling horoscopes that seldom, if ever, provide genuine help and improvement for the client.

OFF-THE-WALL TECHNIQUES

Don't be afraid to use your creativity in developing coaching methodologies and interventions. If your goal is pure—to determine what the actual behavior and results are, and to improve upon them—then your devices may be mainstream, minor stream, or remote creek, so long as they are ethical and legal.

There will be a tonitruous response from the purists and those with "six fundamental steps" in their think kits, but we can leave them to their ranting.

Games

There are superb games on the market that can test an individual's or a team's responses to highly realistic situations and provide both competition and objective results. I was engaged in one of these with a consulting firm, where the CEO and all key personnel were divided among eight teams vying to recruit talent, find clients, run profitable engagements, and repay investors. It took about three hours, and the results were revealing for the individuals, the dynamics, and the strategies. Six of the teams went bankrupt.

Customized Diagnostics

Create a simple diagnostic that enables the client and you to agree on where the client currently is and where he or she would like to be. You can jointly assess behavior after any particular event.

For example, if your goal is to improve prudent risk taking or make better-balanced decisions between risk and reward, you might create something like the scale shown in Figure 5-1.

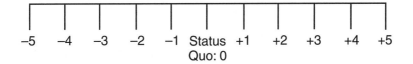

−5   −4   −3   −2   −1   Status   +1   +2   +3   +4   +5
                                Quo: 0

Question: What is the best and worst that might result?

+5 = Paradigm-breaking improvement, industry leader
+4 = Dramatic improvement, major publicity
+3 = Strong benefits, organizationwide
+2 = Minor benefits, localized
+1 = Very minor improvement, barely noticed

−1 = Very minor setback, barely noticed
−2 = Minor setback, controlled locally
−3 = Public setback, requires damage control
−4 = Major defeat, financial damages, recovery time needed
−5 = Devasting losses

Figure 5-1   Risk/Reward Ratios

Help your client to understand the scale's calibrations (and even ask for the client's input), and then use this as a means of assessing whether the client is making decisions with too much risk (e.g., −5 on risk to only +2 on reward) or too much conservatism (e.g., not acting on +4 reward and only −1 risk).

You can create any number of similar diagnostics to enable the client to self-assess, as well, in your absence. (Obviously, many of these are ideal for remote coaching.)

Altering the Environment

I've routinely taken managers who are trying to improve their presentation skills to professional association meetings and even college classrooms to have them present to "stranger groups." This avoids any self-consciousness about having peers in the room, but also provides the requisite pressure to perform well.

You can do the same thing with any number of goals—take someone who is trying to improve sales skills on a call to gain a contribution to a charity, or someone who is seeking better networking skills to an awards dinner (and see how many acquaintances he or she can make while securing contact information).

Create a "Dashboard" for Performance

You may try establishing a control panel or dashboard of critical factors for the client to observe and consider. For instance, the chart in Figure 5-2 indicates what you might do for a client who doesn't act rapidly enough because of a misguided search for perfection.

By having this chart regularly in view, the client can be reminded that at about the 80 percent mark, it's okay to "launch" the initiative or make the decision, with the knowledge that not doing so will create an inordinate diminishing

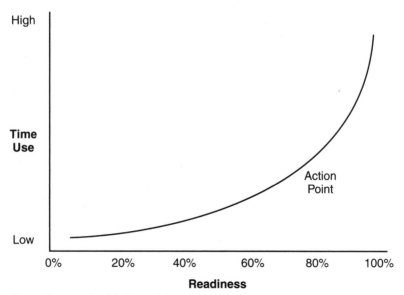

Figure 5-2 Optimal Action Point

return (and that fine-tuning is always available to make the inevitable small corrections).

Create Formal Rehearsals

If a client has a major event approaching (e.g., a board presentation, an acquisition meeting, or a foreign trip), you can assemble people to re-create the scenario. "Mock juries" are common in law school and even during actual major case preparation in large firms.

You may choose to use people from the company if the client is comfortable with this or, if not, use outside resources. This technique is different from the technique of altering the environment in that it seeks to specifically simulate an approaching event or circumstance.

Bring In Situational Experts

Don't consider yourself a "360-degree coach"—that is, one who must know everything about everything. Your client may have some specific issues with image and business etiquette—proper dress or correct dining. Find someone with that particular expertise to help you. (This is why alliances can be quite rewarding when business is actually "on the table.")

You may be helping the client with 70 percent of his or her issues, but others can serve the client better with the remaining 30 percent. (You'll have to anticipate these needs early in the discussions and build in the necessary fees to pay these experts.)

Create Ongoing Self-Assessment

With individuals, and certainly with teams, it's often a great approach to allow the client to assess himself or herself first, before you say or do a thing. The most effective learning always originates with the learner, so give the client a chance to make some observations and analyses.

You can always augment the evaluations, but you'll often find that they are spot-on, which accelerates learning and decreases your own labor intensity. Don't forget, this is part of transferring skills and avoiding codependency.

Don't be afraid to try your own techniques and use your own ingenuity. This can create very appreciative clients, who will then begin to market on your behalf.

PHILOSOPHY AND PONDERINGS ON COACHING

T HROUGHOUT THESE PAGES, I've been rather tough on what I consider to be arbitrary "certifications" and "initials" and "experiences" that somehow qualify you to coach. It's not because all of these offerings are misguided or wrong (although many of them are), but rather because they are too restrictive. I want to elaborate on some of those points and raise some additional ones for your consideration.

If you have the heart to coach, and the willingness to learn from any variety of sources, then the chances are you will be quite good at it and not incidentally, as this book suggests, forge quite a successful business. The dynamic looks like Figure I-1.

Market need:

- What exists: help me to improve my presentation skills.

- What you create: I'll need help using new technologies.

- What you anticipate: how will I lead people I never see in person?

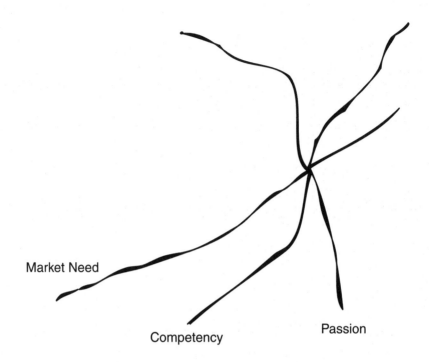

Market Need

Competency

Passion

Where Do These Paths Intersect?

Figure I-1   Three Requirements for Success

Competency:

- What skills can you help me develop?
- What knowledge can you identify that I should acquire?
- What experiences do you suggest that I arrange to undergo?

Passion:

- Can you overcome rejection and objections?
- Can you deal with ambiguity, delay, and events that are out of your control?
- Are you resilient?

These dynamics apply both to you and to your clients. At the confluence of the three, you are in a thriving business, and your client is in a thriving career. Since they apply so universally, *it is worthwhile getting good at them!*

Thus, my issue with diplomas and certificates is that they are artificially restrictive. There are myriad ways to gain these three essential elements, and a plethora of means to help clients develop them. And my point throughout this book is that you've already had valuable experiences that you can put to use, and you possess an array of applicable skills. You simply need to organize and focus them. We're not talking about rocket science here (and even rocket science isn't rocket science any more).

Moreover, the "glorification" of coaching as a pseudo-independent profession, ignoring the setting, the other performers, the organizational dynamics, and so forth, is like launching a rocket by focusing merely on fuel and not on direction.

TEST ME NOT

This brings me to one of the most abused coaching approaches, which is instrumented testing. There are a great many difficulties in predicting human behavior and prognosticating on the results, so here is only a sample:

- *The environment.* We tend to act differently in different environments, and we certainly act differently when we're sitting and taking a test. I don't know how many times my wife has reminded me, "You're not with a client now."

- *The other performers.* These folks are never constant, in terms of both people changing their own demeanor based on what's happening to them that day and the importance of the issues, and new people entering the picture on a regular basis. One performer's actions can greatly influence everyone else's.

- *Nurturing and natural inclinations.* We all have a set of baggage that we consciously or unconsciously carry that influences how we react, despite rationality and even intelligence at times. It can be as addictive as crack cocaine. That baggage is tough to throw off the train.

- *Many tests are "forced choice"* (which of these four alternatives is best or worst for you, and you must choose just one). Sometimes more than one (or all four) meet the criterion, and the more the subject is forced to choose only one among equals, the more likely it is that the result will be inaccurate.

- *Poor or missing validation.* Almost any test you can buy without restriction and use without special training is not going to be highly valid. There will be horoscope-like elements that are hard to disagree with (one actually had on the results, "Ignore those elements which you don't think are accurate"!) and are often so generic as to be worthless. Ideally, tests should be validated for the environment in which they are applied.

- *Distorted intent.* Most tests, even those that are highly regarded and restricted to trained professionals and therapists, were designed to determine if there was aberrant behavior present, *not to discriminate among healthy behaviors.* Consequently, the overwhelming need to provide feedback to healthy people is somewhat different from the intent of winnowing out those who are somehow "damaged."

- *Labeling.* Instead of using results to better understand people, we tend to reverse the process and reduce understanding by dropping people into labeled drawers: "What do you expect from a High D, an INTJ, an expressive expressive?" This is just a centimeter away from asking, "What do you expect from a woman?" or "What do you expect from someone with his origins?" or "What do you expect from people that age?" I've actually been in organizations (not for long) where people's "profiles" were publicly shared "to facilitate communication." They did just the opposite. At one point, the old Providence Gas Company (now part of National Grid) printed people's profiles on their coffee cups, with the idea that the cup was held with the profile facing the other party, so that the behavioral predispositions of the drinker could be read! (I couldn't make this stuff up.) I asked what happened when someone borrowed a coworker's cup. No one seemed to have considered that.

- *Performing to the test.* There is a phenomenon that in public speaking is called "performing to the feedback sheets" and in management evaluations is called "performing to the evaluation." That means that the individual focuses not on goals and performance, but on meeting the criteria in the evaluation and feedback, which are known in advance. This doesn't improve performance; it simply improves arbitrary ratings. In one pharmaceutical company, I found that all managers were measured on a dozen scales, with ratings to three decimal places. In other words, you could have received a 6.134 on a scale of 7.0 for "listening carefully" or "involving others in decisions."

If the company standard were 6.45, then that manager labored mightily to listen or involve and raise that rating by 0.316 come hell or high water. (Customers on the phone? They'll have to wait, I'm listening and involving and shooting for 6.45.)

Notice on LinkedIn sites on July 19, 2010:

"Life Coach Training $697—16 Hr Certification Course live online highly interactive fun Begins Weekly" from the "Institute of Professional Coaching," which prominently advertises: "Become a certified professional life coach in just 16 hours."

I couldn't make this stuff up.

- *Off-the-shelf mediocrity.* Technology is wonderful, but rarely for its own sake. For example, the 360-degree offerings that you can use on the Web are inexpensive, fast, and user-friendly—and in my view not terribly accurate or valuable. Your value as a coach is always greater when you truly customize your approaches for a particular client. If feedback such as what a 360-degree test can deliver is sought, then
  - Determine the information required about the performer.
  - Determine what questions will generate that information.
  - Determine who should be involved (customers, superiors, peers, subordinates, vendors, and so forth).

- Conduct the interviews, listen for patterns, and adjust future questions accordingly.
- Summarize valid feedback for your client and/or buyer.

It's simple but, ironically, far more valuable than using a generic, automated approach.

For these reasons and a host of others, I find that testing is not only overdone among coaches, but often used unethically, without a proper foundation, without proper training and certification, and almost entirely as a revenue-generating alternative. You don't need it, but if you find the appropriate opportunities when you do, use it correctly.

IMPROVEMENT IS AN ELUSIVE TARGET

There are several major areas of potential improvement for your clients. It's important not to confuse them or to use the wrong remedy or timing.

I. *Skills development.* Skills are trainable and learnable. They are best learned on the job, but classroom training and learning materials can do the trick IF there is feedback and prompt application in the real world, with additional feedback. (That's why a coach is more than a teacher and more like a consultant.)[1]

---

[1] Note that all of these CAN be tested for, but these are not personality and behavioral predisposition tests.

II. *Knowledge improvement.* This is the ability to use information in combination to reach goals, solve problems, make decisions, plan, and so on. It's usually developed in two ways:

A. Books and learning aids.

B. On-the-job acquisition of knowledge (which leads to wisdom).

Explicit knowledge (known by the organization and colleagues) must be made implicit so that any individual may access it readily. And implicit knowledge (residing within the individual as a result of on-the-job learning) must be made explicit so that the organization and colleagues are enriched (and don't have to reinvent the wheel).

III. *Experiential opportunities.* There is no substitute for managing an overseas operation, dealing with the customer on the customer's premises, or using technology to remotely communicate with a subsidiary across time zones. This can be arranged and coordinated, but it must be personally undertaken.

IV. *Behavior modification.* Some behaviors can't be "taught" or "learned" in a classroom. In fact, most must be changed through appeals to the client's self-interest, superimposing more positive behaviors on less appropriate ones. Helping someone understand that he is better served by not interrupting subordinates to prove that he knows the answer, because the subordinate will accept more accountability if she is not second-guessed, is an example of trying to modify behavior through such appeals to self-interest.

V. *Therapeutic intervention.* There are some issues that a coach is not suited to tackle, at least not in a coaching capacity, and usually not at all. Borderline behavioral disorders, depression, attention deficit disorders, bullying, and other pathologies demand not only a skilled therapist, but also someone who is not also attempting to improve the person's management or job effectiveness. Once identified, these types of issues should be referred to the company's employee assistance program, a personal physician, a therapist, or some other equivalent professional.

Because of these diverse and sometimes overlapping needs, it's important that you understand your role, your capabilities, and the resources that you can command. I'm always disturbed by "life coaches" who seem to believe that they can help with any issue, no matter what type, through a single methodology (or, all too often, no methodology and merely a lot of opinions).

Note that in Figure I-2, what I "mean" and say you may or may not hear and "get," and vice versa. We have differing

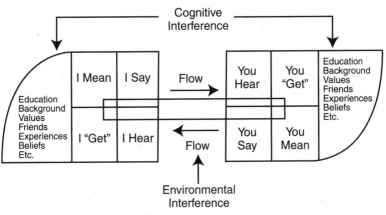

Figure I-2   Communications Flow

backgrounds, education, experiences, and, in this case, roles. Consequently, the obvious environmental interference often overcomes the ability to understand that there is cognitive interference that just might be more distorting and misleading.

In order to choose the proper areas for improvement and the appropriate tools to achieve it, you need to ensure that your client "gets" what you're saying and that you're "getting" what you client says. This is increasingly crucial the more your coaching is remote and infrequent.

THREE DIMENSIONS OF COACHING

From 50,000 feet, the execution of a coaching assignment involves three main dimensions: preparation, delivery, and follow-up.

Preparation

Work with your buyer (whether or not this is also the client) to agree on implementing in accordance with the accepted proposal. This might include

- Confidentiality
- Timing
- Joint and separate accountabilities
- Periodic briefings
- Payment terms
- Access and security
- Nondisclosure agreements
- Mutual contact information and access

Work with your client (whether or not this is also the buyer) to agree on the implementation approaches. This might include

- Start date
- Frequency of visits
- Frequency of remote access
- Confidentiality
- Others' involvement (e.g., 360-degree assessments)
- Variety of intended interventions and their planning
- Ending date intended
- Feedback types and protocols
- Unplanned and impulse possibilities
- How you will be introduced, if necessary
- On-site and/or off-site work
- Documentation intended

You should also prepare yourself. If you haven't done so in acquiring the business, you may want to consider the following in preparation for delivery:

- Reading about the company's founding and history[2]
- Learning about parent or subsidiary companies
- Understanding the company's customers or clients
- Understanding the competition and the company's competitive standing

---

[2] This often has profound impact, as in the iconology around FedEx or Hewlett-Packard's "HP Way" and the founders' famous original garage.

- Understanding the client's position and job accountabilities
- Understanding to whom the client reports and who reports to the client
- Carving out the proper time in your calendar, including "slush time"
- Increasing your knowledge of the company's culture, politics, and "hot buttons"
- Acquainting yourself with company strategy

While some of these may seen daunting, most people love to talk about their jobs, their company, corporate gossip, and so forth. You just have to be willing to ask some provocative questions and listen. And, of course, the Internet makes all kinds of investigative work easier than ever.

Proper preparation makes delivery that much easier.

Delivery

Don't use all the tools in your kit simply because they're there. Choose what makes the most sense in your environment and with your client. For example, interviews are seldom useful in a culture of mistrust. A 360-degree feedback assessment won't work well if participants feel that their remarks might be too easily attributed to them despite promises of confidentiality. If your client tends to default to "good behavior" when you're observing an evaluation, scheduled and direct observation may not be utilitarian.

Try to vary what you do, with some tools scheduled and some on impulse. That way, you'll tend to get an accurate and realistic cross section of your client's behavior. Plan for formal feedback sessions, but also provide ad hoc feedback when it is most timely and will have the greatest impact. Make sure that you provide positive reinforcement at critical junctures.

When I cited "slush time" in the discussion of preparation, I'm anticipating that there will be unplanned interruptions and interference in your delivery that are unavoidable, and that may otherwise disturb your schedule. Simply arrange to compensate for them.

Give your client time to allow you to observe, listen to your feedback, try to adjust behavior, and get more feedback. Some things can be done quickly (don't hold your notes in your hand when you speak), and some things take a while and repetition (don't lose your temper when subordinates start blaming each other).

Make certain that you are measuring gradual progress. Don't wait until the end of the designated time frames and expect a metamorphosis.

Follow-Up

Many people talk of the importance of "disengagement," and I discuss it in the book. But I'll also suggest that your client is a human being who has relied on you for critical assistance. Therefore, it's both difficult and inappropriate to merely "cut the cord" at some arbitrary point in time.

Ideally, you can build some follow-up into the options in your proposal. That will provide for an expected and structured approach for which you're compensated for 30, 60, or 90 days or whatever.

Short of that kind of formalized follow-up, you can also do the following, which should further improve your relationship with your client and your buyer:

- Call your client once a month for the next 90 days and offer to listen and provide brief reactions to his or her progress.

- Offer to respond to e-mail for 30 days following the engagement's end.
- Put your client in contact with other clients in a chat room or Web site.
- Provide a free quarterly teleconference for clients.
- Provide a monthly electronic newsletter for clients.
- Offer to stop by for a visit if you have other projects within that organization.

You should also make sure that you periodically follow up with your buyer, if not the client, to explore other clients, referrals, testimonials, and so forth. Keep the buyer on your mailing and call lists. It's far easier to obtain business from existing (or past) happy clients than it is to create new clients.

A coaching engagement is finite, *but a client relationship is not.*

OBSTACLES

I'm optimistic as a rule, and I believe that we all grow by building on strengths rather than focusing on the remedial—constantly improving minor imperfections. However, there are two major types of obstacles that bear some consideration: self-imposed and client-imposed.

Self-Imposed

The greatest obstacles are the ones that we create. For example, the rubric "specialize or die" is so inordinately conservative, restrictive, and factually incorrect that I scarcely know where to begin with it. Why wouldn't you offer as diverse a range of services as your market, competencies, and passions allow? Yet we allow this pseudo-advice (inevitably from unsuccessful people) to intrude upon our paths to success, creating time-consuming detours and sometimes career-ending breakdowns.

Here are the most common self-imposed obstacles to success in coaching that you can prevent or correct now that you're aware of them:

1. *Overreliance on a single methodology.* Every coaching client is different. They may fall into patterns, but the person, environment, needs, and so on occur in varying combinations. Don't seek to superimpose a "four-step" or "three-week" or "boot camp" program. Listen to the needs, formulate a tailored approach using only those tools that make sense, and create your intervention.

2. *Focusing on inputs, not outputs.* Goals and behavioral change and business results are the point, not days spent, time invested, or experiences endured. Take a look at your Web site and collateral material. Listen to your own conversations. Are you stressing *what you do* or *how the client improves?*

3. *Failing to blow your own horn.* If you don't blow your own horn, there is no music. It's a myth that no one wants to admit to having used coaching help. It's now a sign of strength and confidence. Solicit testimonials and endorsements, and try to get some of them on video for your Web site.

4. *Being a herd animal.* A psychologist who approached me for mentoring help actually had 14 initials on his card after his name, and I recognized only "Ph.D." The others not only mystified me, but made me suspicious, since they appeared to be begging me to

believe that the credentials equaled talent. A coaching university "diploma" or "certificate" is a piece of paper, and no executive client cares about it. Don't be part of the herd; stand out through your value and relationships.

5. *Failure to market.* This is a marketing business more than a coaching business. That is, you don't get to coach unless you market successfully. If you don't do this well, you'll wind up as someone else's subcontractor, and that's not a route to million dollar coaching (or even six-figure consulting). This isn't the "dirty" part of the business; it's the essential aspect that all great businesses and professions engage in, from Apple to Southwest, from McKinsey to your local accounting firm.

Client-Imposed

1. *A failure to agree internally.* This occurs when the buyer and the client are different people, the buyer recognizes the importance of the client's improvement, and the client provides disingenuous support to minimize any conflicts. However, once you start, it becomes clear that the client isn't going to cooperate. This can be avoided by meeting the client before the proposal is submitted, being candid, and testing responsiveness. It can be corrected if it is missed originally by going back to the buyer and explaining that only the buyer has the "clout" to enforce compliance by the client. (This is also why you should always try to be paid in advance.)

2. *Interfering priorities emerge.* These are inevitable and can't be prevented. An acquisition or divestiture

is announced, or a key client is threatening to leave your client, or a new technology is introduced by the competition. Don't attempt to swim against a riptide. Swim to the side and point out that the very needs of your client are more urgent than ever in these crisis or high-opportunity conditions, and what better environment could there be in which to build and apply new skills and behaviors? Don't be shunted aside; make your work more important than ever.

3. *Other parties contribute to the issue.* You may find that your client's attempts to improve are affected by others who may have very different agendas. For example, in trying to help your client run better meetings, you may find that he is confronting peers from another department who have conflicting interests and are obstructionist. These kinds of "uncontrolled" events may require the intercession of your buyer (if this is not your client) to approach the others, or a modification acknowledging that this particular situation requires special treatment. Your client can still improve, no doubt, but the improvement may not be as dramatic, given the others' private interests.

4. *Unrealistic expectations.* You can't turn a mumbling presenter into Socrates or Henry Clay overnight. You need to set metrics with your buyer and your client so that improvement and not perfection is the goal. Never focus on "ratings" from others (such as evaluation sheets after a speech), since they are notoriously tainted by irrelevant factors (one's commute, the lighting, priorities waiting back at the office), but rather focus on observed behavior: "You

handled questions well by repeating them, providing an answer in less than 30 seconds, and then checking to see if the questioner was satisfied."

5. *Insufficient observational opportunities.* You can't coach someone by sitting in her office or sharing lunch. You have to watch her (which is why testing instruments are so overrated). Make sure you're creating, with your buyer, a regimen where you can see the client in action. If you're told that you can't accompany her to clients or can't watch him give evaluations or aren't allowed on the plant floor, then what are the options left? When one buyer told me that the company's busiest season was approaching, which was quite hectic, so access would have to be limited, I pointed out that this was the best time to be coaching and in the midst of things. What was the alternative—to watch the client when nothing was happening?!

COACHING AS A BUSINESS

Million Dollar Coaching isn't meant to be a mercenary title, but one that serves metaphorically to demonstrate that you can establish a great *business* in this profession, one that allows you to create vast wealth (discretionary time), help others, and achieve higher levels of personal growth.

However, coaching must be seen as a business. It isn't a "calling" unless you intend to do it for free. My wife and I had two friends that we would occasionally see socially. My wife and the other woman knew each other both personally and professionally. Her husband was a counselor who ran his own practice with a partner. He maintained two offices and a small staff, turned no one away, and took whatever payment was offered, no matter how little, also focusing on areas where schools and government provided very low reimbursement.

He could easily have diversified his practice to include more higher-paying clients. They had two children of their own. Instead, he ignored finances, assumed that his wife's job would make up any differences needed between income and expenses, and simply indulged in his "calling." Today, after a very bitter divorce, she is trying to establish herself in another city, and he is doing the exact same thing.

Do not confuse avocation and occupation. The former is a joy, hobby, pastime, and passion that some people are able to turn into an occupation (a toy train lover opens a store, someone who loves cars opens a repair shop). The latter is *also* involved with your passion, but additionally can generate money through your competence and the significant market need that exists or that you create. (That's why virtually no kids who open curbside lemonade stands make money—there's insufficient traffic!)

There are many professions where you find very poor business practices: doctors who schedule back-to-back appointments with no flexibility; lawyers who ridiculously charge in six-minute increments instead of for their value; architects who charge by the hour by focusing on their deliverables instead of results; teachers who join unions that stress longevity on the job instead of outcomes for the students. These are lofty professions, requiring advanced degrees in many cases.

Yet these professionals regard themselves as hourly services providers, implementers, and/or blue-collar workers.

The solution that will break this mindset for yourself in coaching is to develop a strong brand. A brand is a uniform representation of quality, and the ultimate brand is your name ("Get me Alison Nash"). Accompanying that brand is your expertise. Both your brand (or brands) and your expertise should constantly be growing. Too many coaches are stuck in a rut—a success trap—and cease growing.

In Figure I-3, the top left quadrant shows an "authority," someone who has great expertise *and who is widely recognized to possess it.* In this book's chapters I point out that people such as Marshall Goldsmith, Jeff Gitomer, Seth Godin, Marcus Buckingham, and I are seen as "authorities" who are at the top of certain "niches" (however broad those niches may be). In a study I participated in for the National Speakers Association several years ago, we found that true buyers are most drawn to expertise, and therefore that expertise had to be manifested as prominently as possible.

In the upper right, we have those with a powerful brand, but no expertise: "empty suits." These are smooth talkers, perhaps, but without content. Picture the "pitchman" at the car-

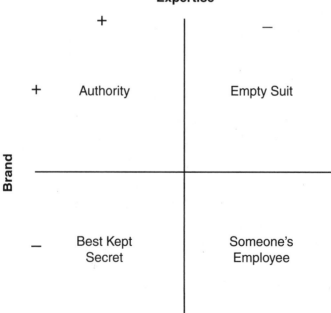

Figure I-3 Combinations of Brand and Expertise

nival, or all those infomercials telling you how you can make a billion dollars in real estate in the next 24 hours if you buy a $19.95 book ("but wait, there's more!").

In the lower left, we have too many coaches: they are very adept, but no one knows about them and they are reluctant to blow their own horns—they have no brand; there is no music. That is where most readers of this book will find themselves (except for those who are already in the upper left and want to make sure they stay there). This is what happens when you view your work as an avocation and not an occupation.

In the bottom right is a nine-to-five worker, a fate from which we are all trying to escape.

As you read this book and/or reread parts of it, keep these facts in mind. You need good methodology, but outstanding marketing, not the other way around. That may sound strange and even alien at first.

But the reason I've been such an effective coach is that, while I'm passionate about the work, I never lose site of the reality that this is a business and I must always act as a businessperson.

You can't help others unless you successfully help yourself.

CREATING LONG, LONG-TERM CLIENTS

ONCE YOU'RE IN, WHY GO OUT?

MARKETING LATERALLY

There is an old and particularly dumb mantra in this business that's usually stated as, "You can't market and deliver at once." Here's why it is so particularly ignorant: it would mean that the more you work, the less you can develop future work, so the less you'll ultimately work. So working will decrease work.

What?

This is one of those facile phrases that are created by empty-headed "experts" to assuage their own weaknesses. Just because they don't know how to market and deliver concurrently doesn't mean that it can't be done! (In psychology, *transference* means that if I had trouble learning to serve in tennis, then you must too, or else you have abilities that I don't have, and I really don't want to consider that.) There are all kinds of utterly nonsensical rubrics like this, such as, "Never dress better than your client," or, "Charging by time units is the best way to judge income," or, "Divide your expense needs into the hours you want to work and you'll arrive at your hourly rate."

These are deadly pseudo-beliefs, and they are not the road to million dollar coaching. They are the road of the herd, mindlessly traveling the savanna searching for food.

If you're dealing in major markets, about 70 to 80 percent of your business should be either repeat or referral (and in small markets, where repeat business is more difficult because of the market size, about 50 percent should be referral). But you need to develop that business while you're there, at the client. Absence does not make the heart grow fonder; it makes people forget.

> *Stop It! You're not "selling," and you're not trying to "take money" from your buyer. You have value that is vital to the client, and it's incumbent on you to make that value available in as many forms and to as many people as possible.*

When you are on a client site, you will meet people. Be sociable and gracious. Meet potential recommenders and buyers. Yes, your work is often confidential. But I'm not suggesting that you reveal what you're doing; instead, find out what others may need.

Some examples of lateral marketing follow. By "lateral marketing" I mean reaching out to other buyers while you're working within a client.

Ask Your Client and/or Buyer

Within the bounds of whatever confidentiality you may be operating, ask if others can benefit from this same type of development. Specifically:

- If this is part of a program that takes place at given points in an employee's career, how can you be considered as an ongoing resource? Point out the benefit of a common approach and the lack of any need to "reeducate" you in the organization's culture and systems.

- If this isn't a team assignment, is the client part of a team that can clearly also benefit, or has the work turned up evidence that the client can't completely meet developmental goals without team involvement?
- Inquire about the various people included in any 360-degree assessment work. Would they be candidates for coaching?

If You Are Doing 360-Degree Assessments, Do Others Show Interest?

Ask permission of your buyer to follow up with any members of the interview group who voluntarily ask about the work and inquire as to whether they could be similarly helped. Don't forget that coaching is often seen as a major developmental effort that is done for high-potential people.

Accent the developmental, not the remedial, aspects of coaching.

At Meetings You Attend, Be Alert for Opportunity

As part of your assignment, you may attend a meeting where a key executive makes a horrible presentation. You may observe evaluations where the recipients are terribly unprepared for how to accept feedback and make self-assessments. You might observe inappropriate treatment (or great treatment) of customers.

What are you seeing and experiencing that may create opportunities for your client to improve still more by using your help still more?

If Confidentiality Is Not a Factor, Be Bold

You can be recognized as a coach without divulging whom you are coaching. If that's permissible, the company publications, intranet, and other sources may be interested in an interview, an article, a podcast, or something similar.

You can help the organization create a culture of coaching and support, and you may even get your buyer and your client to endorse what you've done. In many cases, a senior manager will serve as the exemplar, explain the importance of his or her personal coaching, and then urge subordinates to similarly engage in the development. When that occurs, people jump on board!

When you're in client meetings, or presenting findings, or simply chatting with colleagues, here is the "power marketing language" that you'll find useful. Remember, you're not boasting, you're enabling others to access your value.

- "Here are the most dramatic differences I've found in people who use coaching on an ongoing basis versus those who are never coached or who engage someone only once."

- "Our lives and careers change, and coaching is important to reconsider as conditions continue to evolve. We're seldom the same people we were even two years ago."

- "The people who provide the most dramatic improvement for organizations are the all-stars, the top performers, yet they are the ones who are most seldom coached."

- "One of the major benefits of using outside resources for coaching is that they can objectively introduce external best practices and help assemble internal best practices."

- "The best coaches transfer skills, so that important issues are resolved and the means to resolve them become resident within the organization."

You get the idea. These are not sales situations; you've already been hired, and you're delivering. But you're also marketing laterally so that you create long-term clients.

Always think of the fourth sale first. By that I mean, think of the long-term benefits you can provide the client and how best to position them. That might mean making decisions about where you start, with whom, under what conditions, and for how long. You may want to work with a key manager who can influence others, or a skeptic whose endorsement would be profound, or a person charged with a highly visible new venture.

These days, it's a badge of honor to be using a coach. It's no longer a sign of a need for remedial help, but one of someone deemed to be a key player. That can lead to a variety of interesting routes to travel.

MARKETING IN A "WEB" SYSTEM

You're seldom merely in a client organization. Your buyer has peers, subordinates, superiors, vendors, customers, and so forth. You are actually part of a business ecosystem, and you need to start viewing this "web" in an innovative manner.

Just like the Web of the Internet, the business/social/ cultural web of your client comprises varying relationships that interact situationally, but can be sparked into action through the stimulus of a single source. For example, it's not unusual for a major manufacturer to tell all its component parts suppliers that they must undergo training in quality principles that the manufacturer is installing (or lose out on future contracts). It's increasingly common for companies to host Web sites where they encourage customers to talk to the company and even to each other, no matter how negative some of the feedback may be. (This strategy enables the company to get credit for hosting the forum, and to respond to unfair critiques and learn from accurate critiques.)

Parent companies dictate terms to their subsidiaries, but subsidiaries are sources of ideas (and profit) for the parent. Organizations and their people belong to professional and trade groups, form alliances, and sometimes merge. In many organizations, the customers have customers (wholesale and retail).

Thus, you must be aware of the relationships of your buyer/client and of the immediate organization (the division, department, or office in which you're engaged). You can sometimes develop much "safer" referrals to distant parts of the web. In other words, a client might not want to divulge to a close colleague that you provided coaching, but will feel quite comfortable recommending you to a distant division or a colleague in a professional association.

To engage in this weblike thinking, you ought to chart the client and the organization's relationships as you learn of them, and also do some homework. Here are some sources:

- Ask about the trade and professional associations in which individuals represent the organization.
- Listen for information about who are the best customers.
- Listen for information about suppliers and vendors.
- Track people you meet who are transferred or placed on special assignments.
- Investigate the various teams, task forces, and committees that your client may be part of.

- Talk to your buyer about other, similar people who are under his or her purview and might require similar help.
- Observe major meetings and learn who attends and what units they represent.
- Inquire about overseas operations (you never know!).

There is a second, more immediate web to be sensitive to, and that comprises the people around you in your coaching assignment. This is larger than you may at first imagine, and I've charted a typical example in Figure 6-1 so that you can see what I mean.

You are the coach in the center of this universe. Figure 6-1 shows two current buyers whom you are coaching or whose subordinates are your clients. They may have other subordinates who have similar needs. However, they may also have col-

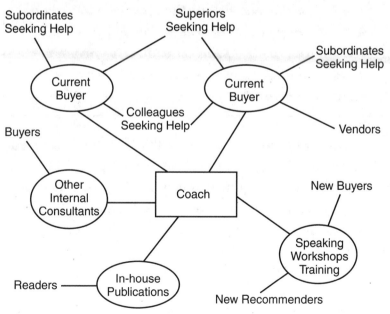

Figure 6-1 Web Marketing

leagues with similar needs, and those other buyers will have a range of new subordinates who could benefit from your value.

Buyers also have vendors and suppliers, who in turn will have buyer/client potential for you. If you provide some training or workshops within the client, that opens the door to new buyers and new recommenders. Most organizations have in-house publications (often called "house organs"), either in hard copy or electronic. Writing an article or being interviewed will open up new interest in your work. And even internal consultants, employees of the client organization, may find you a very useful alliance partner, offering skills and value that are not resident within the business.

I've kept the chart simple for the purposes of our discussion. If you envision it in three dimensions, you can see that the relationships can be quite complex and represent significant potential. Most coaches don't bother to even look!

> *Stop It! Your world within the client is more than merely what you can see every day. Explore the breadth and depth of the relationships around you and you'll find vast opportunities for continuing business.*

This is why I advise looking at the "fourth sale first" and taking a comprehensive view of client relationships. And it's also why I can so easily advocate that upwards of 70 percent of your business should be referral or repeat business.[1] Too many coaches fall into a syncope when they hear that they should be actively looking for these kinds of marketing opportunities while they are engaged with a client. But it makes eminent sense.

---

[1] *Referral* means that a buyer promotes your services to another buyer, and *repeat* means continuing business from the same buyer.

If you feel that you offer great value, and you're already helping people within the client organization, doesn't it make sense to spread and intensify that value while you have the momentum and while you're interacting with your buyer?

When coaches fail to do so, it's because of self-esteem issues and a belief that a sale is some kind of adversarial process. So, even for their sake, let's look at how you can draw people to you who beg you to help them!

MARKETING GRAVITY

About 15 years ago, I created the "gravity dynamic," illustrating the alternatives available for professional services providers to attract buyers to them. This attraction is important for two essential reasons:

1. When people come to you and seek out ways to work with you, then you needn't worry about proving how good you are, establishing credentials, and so forth.
2. Fee becomes an academic discussion, because value is the overarching consideration.

We have two basic mechanisms for acquiring clients: "reaching out" and market gravity. Early in your career, you'll need to depend more on reaching out. But even then you should begin to install market gravity components. At a certain point in your career, you should be relying on the gravity effect for at least 80 percent of your leads and business. Some of us, with strong brands and repute, rely upon it 100 percent. I can't remember the last time I did any "outbound" marketing of any kind.

You can start with just a few components, within your comfort zone, then evolve into those that are less comfortable.

The more routes you set up for people to reach you, the more probable it is that you'll have a full pipeline.

> **Stop It! You really never know where your next lead or recommendation will come from, so don't worry about "number of hits" or other metrics. All you need is ONE HIT to justify the existence of any of these avenues of attraction.**

Gravity will attract people to your Accelerant Curve, which we'll discuss in a later chapter. Over the years, the components of market gravity have shifted and changed along with technology, perceptions, society, and so forth. But for now, Figure 6-2 shows the current "snapshot" in the evolution.

Starting at "12 o'clock" on the chart, here are very brief explanations:

1. *Pro bono work.* This isn't "dialing for dollars" for a charity. Volunteer for board or committee work for a nonprofit whose cause you believe in, and you'll be a peer (by dint of your presence) with the vice presidents and general managers working alongside you.

2. *Commercial publishing.* Write a book, or columns, or articles for a third party (hard copy or electronic for the latter two). Get the tacit endorsement of editors and publishers who print your ideas.

3. *Print interviews.* Through sources such as PRLeads.com or ExpertClick.com, you can arrange to have access to reporters and assignment editors who may seek you out for your expertise for both print and broadcast purposes.

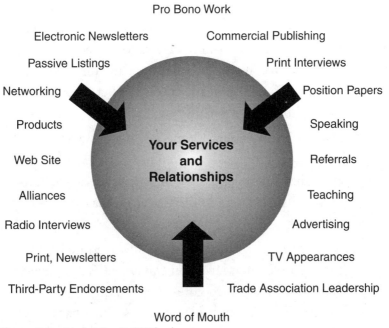

Pro Bono Work

Electronic Newsletters   Commercial Publishing

Passive Listings   Print Interviews

Networking   Position Papers

Products   Speaking

Your Services
Web Site   **and**   Referrals
Relationships

Alliances   Teaching

Radio Interviews   Advertising

Print, Newsletters   TV Appearances

Third-Party Endorsements   Trade Association Leadership

Word of Mouth

Figure 6-2   Market Gravity™ Wheel

4. *Position papers.* Create two- to five-page "white papers" or position papers on subjects related to your coaching value, nonpromotional, that can be posted on your Web site and placed in your press kit.

5. *Speaking.* Speak wherever you find recommenders and buyers in the audience. Many groups will pay you, but that's inconsequential (unless you're also a professional speaker). Get your message out to a roomful of prospects at one time.

6. *Referrals.* Learn language such as this, and use it at least quarterly with all key contacts: "Referrals are the coinage of my realm. Do you know of anyone who can use the value I provide, as you're familiar with it? Would you be agreeable to introducing me or allowing me to use your name?" If you don't ask, you don't get.

7. *Teaching.* By teaching in a local college or university, as an adjunct professor in the evening, you'll meet mostly adults who can refer you to business or even hire you. You'll also gain publicity in your field (e.g., influential communications, or conflict resolution, or general business coaching).

8. *Advertising.* There are some rare venues where advertising can make a difference—for example, specialized newsletters and magazines that you know your prospects read in their professional or personal interests.

9. *TV appearances.* These are generally overrated, and most people interviewed on *Oprah* or *Good Morning America* who are corporately focused don't dramatically improve their business. But a hard news show with a demographic that matches your buyers can make sense.[2] A good source where you can both advertise (point 8) and appeal to talk show hosts is Radio-TV Interview Report (RTIR): www.rtir.com/index.html.

10. *Trade association leadership.* If you take an officer's position, especially the top position, you will be the one who is interviewed and pursued about your organization's goals and impact. The time investment can provide important returns for you.

11. *Word of mouth.* Viral marketing is very powerful. Some people will advocate for the social media platforms. I'd suggest more focused work with colleagues who mention you in key groups in return

---

[2] DO NOT purchase your own time on a cable show or pay to "host" an AM radio show. These are scams.

for your reciprocity. Also, make sure that you "seed" clients into any prospect meetings that you host.

12. *Third-party endorsements.* Testimonials are extremely powerful, since they appeal to peers. Make sure that the name, title, and company are always included (with permission, of course). Video testimonials of about 30 to 60 seconds on your Web site are very effective.

13. *Print, newsletters.* Sometimes a hard-copy newsletter can be more distinctive than an electronic one. People enjoy "quick hit" items about their interests. The key is consistency: same format, same publication date, same "look" every time.

14. *Radio interviews.* See points 3 and 9. You can splice these together (they can run from 5 to 60 minutes) and create a download or CD for future interviewers.

15. *Alliances.* Find those people who lack what you bring to the table. Don't merely conceptualize; wait until there is serious business to discuss. Alliance partners with whom you reciprocate can be a long-term source of gravity.

16. *Web site.* Remember that this is a credibility statement. But involve people. Have downloads; audio, video, and text; self-tests; products; archived newsletters; and so forth. Make it a place that people both return to and tell others about because of the evolving value (see point 11).

17. *Products.* Create products that range from free to costing significant amounts of money, since they will accentuate your brand and are an "easy entry" for strangers. We'll see how this works in detail with the Accelerant Curve later on.

18. *Networking.* Network among strangers who don't have preconceptions, and in places where you're likely to meet high-level buyers: awards ceremonies, political fund-raisers, charity events, arts groups, and so on. Do NOT network with other consultants.

19. *Passive listings.* These are not ads, but lists of specialties that can be found in places such as ExpertClick.com, mentioned earlier. They may be even more useful in specialized publications appealing to your buyers.

20. *Electronic newsletters.* These are simple to create and send, should be no longer than one screen, and should have several different items to try to appeal to the widest population. As with a hard-copy newsletter, consistency in look and distribution is key.

Those are 20 gravity measures, to which you can add still more (blogs, press releases, and so forth). How many are you using? You may find only half of these appealing, which is fine, but if you find few or none of them appealing, then you're in the wrong business.

DIVERSIFYING YOUR COACHING

Coaching is a process. The methodologies we've been discussing can be applied cross-functionally, cross-hierarchically, and cross-culturally. There is no restriction on how they can be applied, except for your own volition.

I've coached police superior officers, CEOs, general counsels, chief financial officers, fund-raising professionals, members of the clergy, executive directors of nonprofits, performers, other coaches, editors, and start-up entrepreneurs, to name just a few of my clients. My methodologies are consistent, but slightly altered to fit the person and the position.

You'll find that you can use the same methodologies for lower-level and higher-level people. However, the fees will vary, since the impact will be different. Your successful coaching of an executive vice president who is responsible for 2,000 people and has a $20 million budget has far more impact than your successful coaching of a supervisor with a $100,000 budget and five people.

The more buyers to whom you can appeal, the more chances there are that your pipeline of prospective clients will be filled. Picture a fishing fleet trying to feed a town by using a mile-wide net or by using individual lines. There are some people who claim that you "specialize or die," but I don't buy that for a moment.

You generalize and thrive.

You should diversify your appeal to the extent that a wide spectrum of potential buyers finds your value attractive. The more adjectives you use, the more you tend to squeeze yourself out of existence, like the 1950s science fiction classic, *The Amazing Shrinking Man*.

Question: What do you do?
Response: I coach people in sales.
Question: What kind of sales?
Response: Telemarketing.
Question: In what area?
Response: Real estate.
Question: What type?
Response: Commercial.
Question: We don't need that.

The more adjectives, the more you "shrink." Here's a different approach.

Question: What do you do?
Response: Dramatically decrease sales closing time and cost of acquisition.
Question: How do you do that?
Response: Share with me your greatest areas of sales need, and I'll give you an example of how we'd work together.

In the second example, the coach focused not on the task but on outcomes, and moved to talk about the prospect's exact sales needs so that the responses would address those very real priorities. The first allowed the prospect to quickly determine that the inputs were not appropriate. The second allowed the coach to demonstrate that the outputs were highly relevant.

> *Stop It! Never focus on the methodologies of coaching. Focus on the salutary results of successful coaching.*

Diversifying your approach is important because your market is like a hydraulic system—when something goes down, other things go up. If natural resources are down, technology might be up. If the private sector is down, nonprofits may be up. If small business is down, the Fortune 1000 may be up.

Why limit your approaches to a sliver of the potential market? Here are some possible surprises:

- Small businesses collectively are the largest employers in the United States, and usually elsewhere as well.
- Nonprofits usually have money, despite their whining to the contrary. Not only do they have healthy

budgets in many cases, but they have boards and donors who can subsidize the operation and write checks.

- Government is a major user of external resources, and in the United States the Federal Acquisition Regulation (FAR) Act stipulates that purchasing need not be based on the lowest price but may be made on the basis of *highest value*.

- Nonprofits can have very professional developmental objectives. Management guru Peter Drucker once wrote that the Girl Scouts was the best-run organization in the United States.

- The "retail" market is very vibrant, and when corporate work declines, the self-help market usually rises dramatically (hydraulics at work). Coaching is a profession that can thrive in both wholesale (corporate) and retail (individual) markets.

And here's another fact that shouldn't surprise you but is often overlooked: the best prospects are already doing well! Don't get caught in a "remedial trap," where you're seen as mainly helping subpar performers to improve. The most money resides in organizations that are doing *well*, and most of them are accustomed to using external resources as needed.

Diversify your offerings, your speech, and your promotional efforts to embrace the widest possible array of prospective buyers. Marketing your coaching services is not like an "on/off" switch, but rather is a rheostat. There are gradations. (New Hampshire has a license plate that states, "Live Free or Die." I've often thought that's a bit extreme, too polarizing. How about, "Live Free or at Least Sufficiently to Fight Another Day"?)

Similarly, you should focus most on high performers. They are the ones who can most dramatically advance a business, in whom continuing investments are made, and from whom the most dramatic returns should be seen in the shortest time. If you get the reputation of doing merely remedial work, you'll be isolated from this rich vein of prospective clients. Seldom do key executives want to be seen as needing help to "fix" them. They prefer to be seen as assets demanding and deserving continuing investment from the organization.

You're better off being "The All-Stars' Coach" than "The Fix-It Coach."

Ignore the people who tell you to find a niche and try to be the big fish in the small pond. Marshall Goldsmith, a colleague of mine and one of the finest and most sought-after coaches in the world, is not measured or interpreted in a niche. He's simply seen as a great coach who can transcend any particular content or environment.

PROVIDING LONG-TERM, ALTERNATIVE SUPPORT

Coaching is a process, not an event. Thus, it occurs over an extended period of time, which might be a month or a year or even longer.

So what's the difference between an extended consulting relationship and the disengagement that we've discussed to avoid codependency? If a client is "constantly" being coached, isn't that the sign of a lack of learning?

Fortunately, no. *Retainer relationships* are expressly designed for longer-term help, and they may last for years. I coached the president of a major subsidiary for five years on an annual retainer. The reasons that you can provide legitimate long-term support include the following:

- The client changes assignments, is promoted, or moves to a new venue.

- Company conditions change (acquisition, divestiture, new markets).

- Technology and communications change.

- Demographics and customers change.

- Global conditions change.

- Societal conditions change.

- Personal circumstances and relationships change.

We all grow older, maturing at different rates. I first saw Tevye sing "Sunrise, Sunset" in *Fiddler on the Roof* with my wife when we were in our twenties, married with no children. We've seen it through the years to the point where our own children have left home, and I am now older than Tevye! That changes one's perspective and can require changed behaviors at work and in life.

The best way to provide longer-term assistance is in a retainer relationship, but I'm using *retainer* in the consulting sense, not the legal sense. The latter is merely a deposit from which hourly charges are deducted, and when it is exhausted, the retainer is replenished. The former is payment for access to your smarts. You gladly pay for an insurance policy, a sprinkler system, and a fire extinguisher, even with the concurrent hope that you'll never have to use them.

The same applies to access to your smarts in a consulting/coaching-type retainer. The client is paying to know you're there if needed. Over those five years with my CEO client, he would call once a month or twice a month, or sometimes not at all during a month. He wasn't paying for quantity, but for the quality of my advice when he needed it and the security of knowing that the quality was accessible when it was needed.

> *Stop It! Never "carry over" time because a client hasn't used the retainer over some time period. Your client is an adult, and you're not the parent. The insurance company doesn't give a rebate because the insurance was never used.*

If you can manage to get a few of your higher-level clients (low-level clients can't afford this in most cases) to put you on retainer, you will have a significant source of income over a prolonged period *with minimum labor intensity*. The keys for determining the value (and, therefore, the fee) of a retainer are threefold:

1. *How many people have access?* Is it the client, or the client and subordinates, or a team? The more people, the more valuable.

2. *What is the scope?* Are you available during eastern U.S. business hours, or also western U.S. business hours? Are you available on weekends (in preparation for the client's Monday morning board meeting)? Is it by phone or e-mail, or in person as well? If in person, how often?

3. *What is the duration?* A retainer should be for a minimum of a quarter-year and can be much longer. You can charge by the month, e.g., $7,500 or $10,000 depending on the previous factors, but you should get paid at least a quarter in advance and give a slight discount for that benefit. I charged $10,000 a month for a yearly retainer, but discounted the fee to $100,000 for the year in return for full payment at the outset: January 1. That proved to be of mutual

benefit—I had the use of the money, and the client's coaching couldn't be canceled.

Consider longer-term work to create longer-term clients. Once they've invited you in, don't be so quick to grab your hat and go!

HOW NOT TO LEAVE MONEY ON THE TABLE

MOST COACHES OVERDELIVER AND UNDERCHARGE

VALUE-BASED FEES FOR COACHES

If you leave $100,000 "on the table" each year—that is, if you undercharge by that amount annually—after 10 years you will have lost $1 million *that you will never, ever recover.* There is no way to retrieve it. If you have been doing that for a decade, you're a million dollars poorer today.

Of course, you can make sure that you avoid that over the *next* decade.

Billable time units are the dinosaurs of professional services. Charging by the day or hour (attorneys charge in six-minute increments in most cases) not only is very low-margin work, but is actually unethical. Think about it: if the client is best served by rapid improvement, but the coach is best paid by lengthy interactions, even with the highest integrity in the world, there is an inherent conflict.

There are also these serious drawbacks to time-based billing:

- The client has to make an investment decision every time he or she perceives a need for you. "Is this issue worth $700 or $1,500 or $2,500?"
- It's too easy for the client to cancel an engagement for frivolous reasons, since there is no penalty.
- The coach is seen as a commodity, and his or her hourly or daily charges are compared against those of other coaches, even though their talents and experiences may differ vastly.
- The client legitimately asks if some interactions can be eliminated or completed in less time.
- It's either tough to budget, because you do not know how much time is needed, or tough to perform a high-quality job because of the converse—an arbitrary limit on the number of hours because of a budget cap.

Value-based fees have become increasingly popular among solo consultants[1] and are spreading. In 2010, the chief justice of the Australian Supreme Court made a public statement admonishing attorneys to change from hourly billing, which neither represented their own value appropriately nor served clients well. (You can see a video of his comments on my blog: http://www.contrarianconsulting.com/value-based-fees-from-australias-chief-justice, and you can see an interview with the owner of an accounting practice on the difference it made for him at http://www.contrarianconsulting.com/page/2.)

---

[1] I pioneered this concept in the early 1990s. See my book *Value Based Fees* (Hoboken, N.J.: John Wiley & Sons, 2006).

In the coaching profession, you can charge by value and not time units if you follow these steps:

1. Ensure that you are talking to the economic buyer, the individual who has the budget to pay for your value. Remember that this may or may not be the client.
2. Establish developmental objectives: what behaviors and results are to be achieved?
3. Establish metrics of success: what evidence and indicators will be used to assess progress and accomplishment?
4. Establish value: what are the impacts of meeting those objectives?

For example, if you are working with a call center manager to improve his interviewing skills, the objectives might be

- In one interview, determine whether a candidate is a good match for success in the call center.
- Decrease the failure rate of new hires.
- Save the money required for constant hiring and retraining.
- Allow the manager to redirect his time from interviewing to improving the unit's performance.

Metrics might be

- Interviews are reduced to a single session of not more than 45 minutes.
- At interview completion, the manager can complete an assessment form comparing candidate information to performance requirements.

- The decision to hire or not is made within 24 hours.
- Overall, 85 percent of new hires remain on the job for at least a year.

The value would include

- Savings of at least $15,000 annually in interview time and follow-up (reduction of 50 hours at a cost of $300 per hour).
- Savings of at least $400,000 annually based on $40,000 cost to replace and train an employee for each position vacated, with an estimated reduction of 10 such turnovers.
- Improved unit performance because the manager can spend more time on development and has more discretionary time and less distraction.

This kind of interview preparation and coaching might require 20 hours of work over the course of a month. If you're charging by the hour, even at $500, that's $10,000 for the project. But if you're charging based on value and, say, a 10:1 return, that would be a $41,500 project, not even counting the value of the increased performance.

And bear in mind that the savings and improvement are readily annualized!

Stop It! Don't treat yourself as if you're a vendor working by the hour. You're a partner working with the buyer to resolve key issues and charging for those results.

When my "billing basis" has been questioned, I use this language: "My fees are based on my contribution to the results we achieve, with a dramatic ROI for you and equitable compensation for me."

The factors you should consider are

- How much influence and impact does my client have on the results?
- How big is the organization being affected?
- What new revenues and profits or decreased and saved costs are involved?
- What does the buyer (not the client, if the client is different) agree upon as tangible improvements?

The critical nuance here is that you ask the buyer what the objectives, metrics, and value (impact) are, so that the buyer commits to them. I call this step *conceptual agreement*, meaning that you and the buyer reach agreement on the value of the project before you even submit the proposal.[2]

Your coaching help has a profound impact on your client and your client's organization. There is no reason in the world for you not to charge an equitable fee for your assistance in that pursuit. And the good news is that this is entirely in your hands, IF you decide to treat each prospect as a value-based-fees prospect and not default to the antediluvian time-based rates.

That's how you can avoid being a million dollars poorer. If you're a veteran, it's never too late to start. If you're newer to the profession, then it's time to embrace the right habits.

---

[2] You can find sample questions for all of these steps in the Appendix.

THE SMART ART OF THE RETAINER

We discussed retainers briefly in Chapter 3 as representative of one of two billing bases (the other being projects) within value-based fees. We'll talk about them again somewhat later as an important result of the Accelerant Curve (Chapter 8).

For now, let's examine the somewhat nuanced role of retainers, because they are actually one of the portals between consulting and coaching.

I established at the outset that most consultants—and by "most" I mean upwards of two-thirds—have coached at some point in their careers, although they may not have called it that. Coaching has often been mandated by the exigencies of traditional projects—senior people have to be instructed in how to reinforce new skills acquired by subordinates, or evaluate the results of new behaviors, or alter their approaches based on changing technologies and circumstances.

Similarly, coaching projects—which have a defined beginning, middle, and disengagement based on specific developmental objectives—can evolve into long-term retainers. This occurs—and avoids codependency, by the way—when

- The client will be evolving, changing roles, facing new circumstances, and adjusting to new conditions.
- The organization anticipates significant changes and challenges.
- Skills and behaviors that are not called upon too often (e.g., facing the media) happen to arise and require "brush-ups" and fine-tuning.
- Periodic and predictable critical junctures (e.g., quarterly board meetings or monthly trips abroad) necessitate propinquity of support.

> *Stop It! Always give the option for a retainer in your proposals and following traditional projects. The client or buyer may not think of it, but the suggestion—and concomitant value—may be extremely attractive.*

Occasionally, a new client will be entirely appropriate for a retainer from the outset, without a project preceding it. These characteristics usually indicate such an opportunity:

- The client is sophisticated and successful, but recognizes key conditions where help will be needed on an "on-call" basis.
- Your rapport is superb, and the client realizes a huge gain merely from having access to your "smarts."
- A sounding board is needed against which to bounce innovative ideas, assessments of risk, and so forth.
- A reconciler or conciliator is needed to resolve differences among the members of a team.
- A "straw man" is required to test assumptions or serve as "devil's advocate."

The pricing of retainers is dependent on three factors:

1. The number of people who have access
2. The conditions (scope) of access
3. The duration of access

Retainers are like insurance policies, or contingent actions that are put in place "just in case." Most people hope never to have to use their disability insurance, or the sprinkler system,

CASE STUDY: Retainer Power

Having completed two successful projects for a $400 million division of a Fortune 25 company, the president and I agreed upon a retainer of $10,000 per month for a year, with a discount to a net $100,000 if it was paid on January 2. He accepted this, and for the first three years of what would be a five-year relationship (until the division was divested), we would renew with a handshake in November.

At the end of the third year, however, I offered the customary renewal, and he said, "No, not this time." I was immediately staggered that I could have been so blind as to take him for granted and not provide enough responsiveness.

Before I could respond, he said, "Raise it to $135,000. You're providing that much value to me."

For only the second time in my life, I was speechless.[3]

or the reserve generator. But they're present and they're kept in good condition and up to date (one hopes) as an important aspect of intelligent planning and peace of mind.

Retainers are analogous. You are there if needed. In the case study just given, I talked to the president about twice a month by phone and visited every other month for a day or two. He would sometimes call on a Sunday before an unscheduled and sudden board meeting for some role-play practice and advice. He occasionally called during halftime of *Monday Night Football*, not because he was watching the game, but because he knew that I was!

He found it important to know that I was there when he needed me. Once, in five years, he asked me to spend a weekend on his site to facilitate an emergency meeting caused by an internal calamity. I happily did so. Don't forget, the retainer alone for this client amounted to $570,000 over five years, after $150,000 in project work. And I was accountable only to the president.

[3] The first time was in sixth grade, when I was made the youngest lieutenant in the history of the grammar school's "junior police," but I was lobbying to carry a gun and use wiretapping on the fourth graders.

Retainers are a combination of art and science. The science is in the scope and duration, but the art is in your own confidence and calmness. Never "roll over" time because it hasn't been used. You're paid in a retainer for being potentially available, not for time actually utilized. Don't feel that you must "make up" days if none have been used. Don't allow for "scope creep" by allowing others to have access because your own client isn't using much of your time.

The artistry is in realizing that you are a profound value and resource *merely by dint of being available.* As coaches' careers progress, they should be moving more and more into retainer work, thereby decreasing their labor intensity, time, and pounding on their souls. Think about it: if you had a dozen of these occurring at the same time, you could make quite a bit of money with minimal "work." There are no TSA security lines on the way from your bedroom to your den, unless you're sleeping at O'Hare Airport.

The reason so many coaches overdeliver and undercharge is that they don't consider the value of their availability and access. They consider themselves worthy only if they are "doing" something. Yet we all consider the fire department and the EMTs highly valuable and worthy of our tax dollars, while hoping that we never personally have to encounter them.

That's in defiance of "conventional wisdom," and that's another story.

SEPARATING YOURSELF FROM "CONVENTIONAL WISDOM"

The conventional wisdom in the coaching profession is neither conventional nor wise. Nowhere is this truer than in the consideration of fees.

I've heard the following uttered in such places as the main stage of major coaching conventions and conferences:

- Coaches are merely "hired hands," and if they're asked to move furniture or work with other coaches while they are there, that is expected and proper.
- Fees are a matter of "supply and demand," so you raise your fees only when demand exceeds supply.
- The basic fees should be set by an agency representing you.
- Fees should be set based on the length of time you're present: brief visit, half-day, full day, or multiple days.

Since the publisher doesn't want me to write a 400-page book, I'll stop there and deal with the basic lunacy (AKA conventional wisdom).

First, we are highly skilled professionals, not jacks of all trades who show up and happen to coach when we're not balancing a ball on our nose or fixing the drains. Can you imagine your physician finishing an exam early and you suggesting that, since there is some time remaining, the good doctor check the oil in your car?

Second, supply will *always* exceed demand unless you book 350 days a year, and even then you could probably coach two or three times in one day. The key to wealth is to generate discretionary time, not to work yourself to death.

Third, agents and middlemen do not have your best interests in mind, or even the client's best interests in mind—they have *their own* best interests in mind. Many of them want to have a lot of low-priced coaches constantly working so that they can collect a high volume of low commissions. You ARE a hired hand to most bureaus, or, worse, a pack animal.

Fourth, a great 45 minutes is worth far more than a lousy day, right? I think that about sums up the time argument.

> **Stop It! Don't allow others to establish fees, fee policies, or fee terms for you. It is your life; they are your fees; it's your decision.**

Fees are based on value, period. The biggest factor governing how well you create, demonstrate, and charge for value is . . . drum roll . . . your self-esteem. There is a difference between self-esteem (the degree to which you see yourself as worthy) and efficacy (the degree to which you do things well). They can be independent variables.

Think of self-esteem as a verb or action that enables you to arrive at a noun or place called self-confidence. The higher your self-esteem, the more confident you will be, and the more confident you are, the more you will appreciate your own worth and be self-assured in asking for equitable compensation in return for that worth. The more you think you're unworthy—*despite your great skills and abilities (efficacy)*—the harder it will be to charge for even significant value delivered, because you just don't believe you're worth it. (This is basically the problem of the "experts" who advise you to think like a hired hand.)

Figure 7-1 gives a quick tutorial.

In the upper left are people who are highly skilled in coaching and also appreciate their worth and value. That understanding of the value they deliver permits them to charge fees commensurate with the help they are providing on a consistent basis, regardless of the environment or the buyer.

In the upper right are people who have the talents but don't feel worthy and are consequently questioning why they

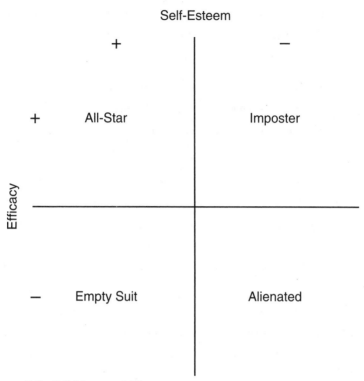

Figure 7-1   Self-Esteem and Efficacy

were chosen or ascribing their success to luck. They feel like imposters who will soon be "found out" by someone. I've met thousands of consultants, coaches, speakers, trainers, and others in related fields who are in this category. They can't charge enough because they feel that they don't deserve it, and that it's only a matter of time before others realize it!

In the lower left, we have the very confident people who have no content, few skills, and limited abilities. This is the "empty suit" or the "cowboy" or the "big hat, no cattle" type that we all cite at various times. Extremely and unjustifiably confident, they can often talk a good game, but, opposite to the imposters, they feel that they'll never be "found out" because they are too glib, too voluble, too charming. They can be uxorious about their profession, but nonetheless poor at delivering on their promises and enthusiasm.

Finally, in the lower right are those who are both without self-worth and without perceived skills. They are alienated and isolated. (There is a type of suicide labeled "anomic," meaning detached from society.)

In all probability, you'll see these types in your coaching work, but you'll also find them among coaches. I mention them here because the only sound way to consistently assess appropriate fees is to be an all-star, with a clear understanding of the skills you bring to bear and an appreciation of how important they and you are in helping your clients.

Unfortunately, the "conventional wisdom" often revolves around beliefs that you should not shine, should not stand out, should not take credit. There are those who will tell you to deliberately "dress down," be careful about the car you drive, and decrease your language sophistication so that the client doesn't feel bad in comparison and/or resent you.

Listen up: powerful people like to be around powerful people. They have sufficient "yes-men" all around them. They are seeking "stretch" and challenge, not more subordinates and obsequious sycophants. If you want to charge high fees based on the value you deliver, then first and foremost you have to recognize and appreciate that value.

The first sale is always to yourself.

DEALING WITH TRUE BUYERS

An essential element in not leaving money on the table is to make certain that you are dealing only with true buyers. These are the people I've been calling "economic buyers" and "true buyers" because they have the authority and the ability to issue a check.

They are *not* identifiable by title or business card in all cases. One of my key buyers at Merck had the title "manager of international development," but had the authority to purchase $250,000 of services with me alone year in and year out. Yet I've met "senior vice presidents" who couldn't validate my parking. (This is particularly true in banks, where *everyone* is a vice president in lieu of being paid decently. At least "sanitary engineers" know, deep within, that they are garbage collectors.)

In a smaller business, the buyer is likely to be the owner or the president. In a larger business, the buyer can be anyone with a proper grant of authority, but it is most likely to be someone with P&L (profit and loss) responsibility: heading a subsidiary, department, or division; head of a key staff function; executive director of a nonprofit; and so forth.

If you're not sure, here are some questions to ask to "flush out" the economic buyer:

- Whose budget will support the investment?
- Who will evaluate the outcome for return on investment?
- Who is the key sponsor or champion?
- Who must approve the final expenditure?
- Whose approval do you need?

You may not use them all, and you certainly won't use them as an interrogation, but if you are bold and determined, you'll find out who really has the money.

Note: Committees don't have budgets; people do. Committees may recommend, but they seldom decide in the corporate world. There are also pseudo-buyers who will tell you that they have the decision-making prerogative, it's their project, and they are the final decision maker. Offer to shake their hand on the premise that, if the two of you reach agreement in the next hour, you can start the project tomorrow. (That's actually a contract.) If they shake, they're probably the buyer; if they don't, they're not. I call this "passing or failing the handshake test.")

The more you take the time to find the economic buyer (who may, don't forget, also be your client), the faster you can obtain high-quality business. You can't allow internal people who are not buyers to do your marketing for you with their superiors. They are never as passionate as you are, they have their own credibility problems, they fear for their future and their retirement plans, and they legitimately can't answer questions about your approaches that only you can answer.

Now, what happens when you actually find an economic buyer? You relate.

Powerful people enjoy dealing with powerful people. Dress well. I'm not talking about "dress for success" platitudes. I mean wear a very good designer suit (Canali, Brioni, Armani, Zenga, and so forth), even if you have to go into hock to buy it. Don't whip out a 19-cent pen. Use a Cartier or Mont Blanc.

Digression

I once requested a diet soda when the buyer offered me coffee, and he had to search the office to find a can, which a secretary gave up with obvious reluctance. As I bolted a drink, the liquid flowed down "the wrong pipe," and it came streaming back out in the direction it had entered. My memory of the buyer was of him wiping used diet soda off a photo of his daughter that had been minding its own business on his desk.

Don't haul in a battered computer bag and 40 pounds of accessories. Use a very good notebook or compact laptop (or tablet, like the iPad). Act as if you're comfortable and quite accustomed to being in large offices and splendid surroundings. Refuse offers of coffee or refreshments, because you really don't need them and the likelihood of spilling them on yourself (bad) or the client (horrifying) is pretty high just by dint of their presence.

Now that you've found the buyer and related to the buyer, what's next? Here are the steps to guarantee that you can deal with economic buyers effectively and never leave money on the table:

1. *Develop a trusting relationship.* This means that the other party believes that you have his or her best interests in mind. That creates trust and sharing. You build trust by offering value, listening carefully, paraphrasing what you hear, and being able to relate to the buyer's experiences and examples (which is why so much of what we do is about intellectual firepower).

   The signs of a trusting relationship are

   • Sharing information that you didn't ask for

   • Asking your advice

   • Laughing at your humor

   • Revealing "inside" information

   • Describing personal (not merely business) objectives

   • Accepting "pushback" and questioning

2. *Seeking the conceptual agreement.* You want to establish the developmental objectives, metrics for progress and success, and impact of meeting the objectives

(value), which I've earlier called *conceptual agreement.* Note that you can't do this effectively until you have a trusting relationship, because the buyer will understandably be loath to share certain information.

3. *Meeting the client if he or she is not the buyer.* It's always useful to see if what you've heard is also what you observe. Is the client amenable to the process and responsive to you? Does the early "chemistry" make sense?

4. *Submitting the proposal.* At this point, and at this point only, you can submit a proposal—preferably with options (a choice of yeses)—to the economic buyer. You've established trust, you have conceptual agreement, and you have met the client.

Options will give the buyer a choice of increasing value (increasing ROI) at higher fees. The offering of options replaces "Should I do this?" with "HOW should I do this?" which will increase your chances of success by at least 50 percent. (If you don't believe this, begin experimenting—don't ask others, "Should we meet again?" but rather ask, "Should we meet tomorrow at the same time, or Thursday for breakfast, or hold a teleconference Friday at 2?")

Finally, true buyers can and will make decisions, so prepare for it. That is, don't merely prepare for obstacles and rejection, but prepare for acceptance and success. You may just hear, "I like what you've had to say, you seem to like us, so how quickly can you begin?" Always take a day to formulate your proposal, or you'll inevitably fail to provide options and underprice your value, meaning that you'll be leaving money all over the table, the chairs, and the floor.

BREAKTHROUGH: MONEY IS NOT A SCARCE RESOURCE

And now the really big news: money is not a scarce resource.

Take a moment.

Along the anfractuous route that many coaches take, from lead to relationship to client acquisition, they are often thrown off a cliff or deposited in a mine shaft because the prospect says, "We'd love to do it, and you are obviously our first choice, but we simply have no budget."

At this stage, the coach will

- Find out a good time to return—say, in six months or a year.
- Ask if there are any other people who may have budget that he or she can meet.
- Attempt to lower the fee!
- Change the terms so that the money isn't payable until the next appearance of Halley's Comet.
- Fold his or her tent and retreat.

All of these actions are ridiculous, and the manifestations of people who do not understand the dynamics of budgeting and expenditures in organizations.

NO ONE wakes up in the morning and suddenly says, "I think I'll put $35,000 aside for a coach whom I've never met but whom I suspect we'll need and who just might show up today." Even when legitimate and anticipated coaching needs are forecast, there often isn't sufficient budget because people can't estimate what the proper fees will be (which is why Human Resources, which never has budget authorization, is always saying, "Can you do it for less?").

Please put a note in the margin at this juncture, or some kind of sticky, bright yellow paper, or your driver's license, because here is an elemental tenet in taking all the money off the table:

Money is not a resource issue, it's a priority issue.

There is *always* money. The lights are on; the employees are being paid; the mortgage is up to date; the insurance is in force. All companies have money.

The question is: to whom will it be paid?

When you hear, "Sorry, we have no money for this project," what you are really being told is, "We have money, of course, but we're not giving it to you because we don't see as much value or return from giving it to you as we do from giving it to other people." Simple as that.

> **Stop It! If you are discussing price and not value, you've lost control of the discussion.**

Coaches either respond to an existing need (help this person to qualify for promotion in the future), create a need (you'll require more technologically sophisticated senior managers), or anticipate a need (I can see where you'll need more help with cross-cultural management once your expansion plans are implemented). Therefore, the establishment of strong needs tied to buyer emotions (logic makes people think; emotions make them act) will raise your standing in the priority list for the money that is floating around the organization.

True buyers, which is why I've been so terribly doctrinaire about dealing only with them, *have the ability to move money from one pile to another*. They have the discretion and the accountability to make wise investments in light of probable returns. They can curtail a conference, or reduce travel, or postpone equipment purchases, or choose not to fill a vacant position. They have all kinds of discretion IF they see a better use for the investment.

Consequently, your approach and your language must be about value and about what the benefits are for the organization, the buyer, and the client or clients. Here is a reminder of the questions from Chapter 2 that can be used to help the buyer appreciate the value of the coaching project:

- What will these results mean for your organization?
- How would you assess the actual return (ROI, ROA, ROS, ROE, or some other metric)?[4]
- What would be the extent of the improvement (or correction)?
- How will these results affect the bottom line?
- What are the *annualized* savings (the first year might be deceptive)?
- What is the intangible impact (e.g., on repute, safety, or comfort)?
- How would you, personally, be better off or better supported?
- What is the scope of the impact (on customers, employees, vendors)?
- How important is this compared to your overall responsibilities?
- What if this fails?

Don't forget, you can apply these in three dimensions (organization, buyer, and client), at least if the buyer and the

---

[4] Return on investment, assets, sales, equity.

client are different people, and beyond that if you are coaching multiple people or teams.

For the bold among you, here are some questions you can ask to ascertain budgetary expectations at the outset of your relationship and/or as you make progress in your discussions:

- Have you arrived at a budget or investment range for this project?
- Are funds allocated, or must they be requested?
- What is your expectation of the investment required?
- So we don't waste time, are there parameters to remain within?
- Have you done this before, and at what investment level?
- What are you able to authorize during this fiscal year?
- Can I assume that a strong proposition will justify proper expenditure?
- How much are you prepared to invest to gain these dramatic results?
- For a dramatic return, will you consider a larger investment?
- Let's be frank: what are you willing to spend?

You might not ask them all, and you might vary your timing and inflection, but you should be searching to make sure that your buyer fully appreciates the value of reaching the developmental objectives and is willing to make a proportional investment in the value to be received.

It's all about ROI.

If you don't want to leave all that money on the table, you're going to have to charge significant fees that represent the value you generate. To do that, you'll have to engage a true buyer in a candid conversation (based on a trusting relation-ship) to establish the tremendous value that will be delivered, so that the fee is an intelligent, rational, and even conservative investment to authorize.

You can't do that with low-level people. You can't do that if you don't use the proper language to focus on value and not price. And you can't do that if you don't believe it yourself.

Remember, the first sale is always to yourself.

AGGRESSIVE MARKETING

YOU, TOO, CAN BECOME A STAR

WHY YOU CAN'T COACH YOURSELF

I have coached time management experts in time management, sales experts in sales, and marketing gurus in marketing.

This is neither surprising to me nor embarrassing to them. You can't coach yourself. And the best of the best receive coaching. (I'm a big believer in therapy, and I periodically seek it, not in response to some trauma or problem, but to explore how well I'm doing and whether I'm seeing the world with the right perspective.)

The best golfers have swing coaches, singers have voice coaches, and business executives have—well, one hopes—you and me! That's why there has been an eternal need for coaching.

However, the lawyer representing himself having a fool for a client (or physician, heal thyself) applies here. If you think about some of the very basics of effective coaching:

- Observation
- Timely feedback

- Trust and "pushback"
- Practice with adjustments

you'll quickly realize that doing that for yourself would result in a professional form of schizophrenia. We are incapable of providing *and receiving* the same quality of coaching for ourselves that we provide for others.

And that is as it should be.

Thus, I'm taking several pages to help you understand that there is a danger in your *not* soliciting coaching help yourself.

You tend to get better and better at what you're already good at. Too many professionals develop a set of skills early (often while learning from others) and then hone and refine and solidify them without acquiring still more skills on a regular basis. Coaching is about lifelong learning, and breadth is even more important than depth.

You fall into bad habits. The client can't usually tell you that you're doing something wrong, or you may simply get lucky and commit an error and get away with it. For example, you might lose contact with your buyer and focus solely on your client, but your buyer gets back in touch with you. That's called being lucky rather than good. Without feedback, it's hard to detect your errors.

The client begins to dictate your methodology. An occupational hazard is simply accepting what the client requests ("We want 60 days of work with the leader of the team because she seems to be out of her element"). This is the equivalent of responding to RFPs (requests for proposals), which are merely someone else's alternatives seeking vendors to fulfill them.

Your frame of reference will always be somewhat restricted. It's always useful to engage with others to understand what else is happening in the profession that simply has not appeared on your radar screen or been possible with your range of clients. Perhaps you've never used 360-degree assessments with clients and it would be useful to learn the pros and cons of doing so.

If you're going to engage in aggressive marketing and seek to become an object of interest, you'll need sounding boards. Just as therapists go through therapy (and some of the best doctors have themselves been patients and learned from the experience), you should engage a coach from time to time.

When I help people understand how to move from six figures to seven figures in income, the most revealing aspect to participants is that they have to radically change the way they do business. As my colleague and über-coach Marshall Goldsmith has said, "What got you here won't get you there." To reach significantly higher levels of performance, income, and discretionary time, you need to dramatically change your business model, which is a natural function of growth.

In finding a coach, you can avoid the dread prospect of unsolicited feedback, which is always, always for the sender. What you need is solicited feedback, which enables you to choose those sources whom you respect and who have the proper expertise and perspective to help you.

What you see in Figure 8-1 is the classic "S curve," which demonstrates that new practices (or products or services) usually have fairly slow growth at first, but, if they are good, rapidly climb. At the top of the S curve, there is a plateau, which I've named the "success trap." That's because the plateau has no growth and, given the laws of entropy, will eventually erode.

Consequently, the time to leap to the next S curve is at maximum acceleration, because that provides the shortest jump

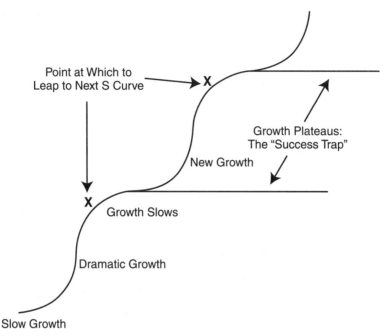

Figure 8-1   The Dynamic of the S-Curve

and the most momentum. If you wait until you're far down that plateau, you've lost momentum, and the gap is enormous.

No company in the vacuum tube business successfully entered the transistor business, which was the immediate technological successor. Motorola was leading the cell phone market by focusing on cosmetics (slimmer and slimmer phones), but it was the combination of technologies that took over the market and knocked Motorola out of it.

Coaching has been affected by globalization, new technologies, societal mores, business strategies, economic shifts, demographic movements, and so forth. Once you're too far down that plateau, you hit the primal scream: "You can't get there from here."

So the journey we're taking from here—helping you become a "star" and a center of expertise, and perhaps a thought leader—is based not on your knowing it all, but on your being willing to continue to learn.

BECOMING AN OBJECT OF INTEREST

I'm differentiating between "an object of interest" and "thought leadership," which is discussed a bit later in this chapter. (And certainly distinguishing it from "a person of interest," who is often found in a police interrogation room with a bare light-bulb and lousy coffee.)

An object of interest (OOI) is someone whom people remark about and often refer to. On the way to becoming a star, you need to achieve some momentum. If thought leadership is the escape velocity, being an object of interest is the initial ignition.

Objects of interest manifest their fascination for others by

- *Providing clarifications and original sources.* Many coaches rely on secondary sources and arbitrary methodologies (coaching "universities") for their approaches. An object of interest will shatter myths. For example, social psychologist Albert Mehrabbian's work is often cited as an example showing that people are influenced more by nonverbal actions than by words. But that conclusion is a distorted interpretation of Mehrabbian's work, which involved people cutting into lines and waiting for service.
- *Appearing frequently in the media.* Through publishing (hard-copy and electronic), interviews, speaking, panels, and other devices, OOIs remain in public view. They comment on trends and make prudent predictions. Someone needs to comment on what the coaching opportunities and limitations are in remote

coaching work, and what different skill sets are required, for example.

• *Being able to make difficult situations and relationships understandable.* They can translate the highly conceptual into the tangible (a process known as *instantiation*). For example, in the graphic in Figure 8-2, we see movement from a current state to a desired state[1] through an uncertain period. The point is that the future can always be made to look desirable, but it's much more difficult to help people (and coaching clients) undertake the journey. It's much easier to visualize this than it is to simply ponder it or try to explain it.

• *Not becoming "lost in the clutter and cacophony."* An OOI tries to set himself or herself apart. OOIs are more pragmatic than conceptual and aren't distrait or lost

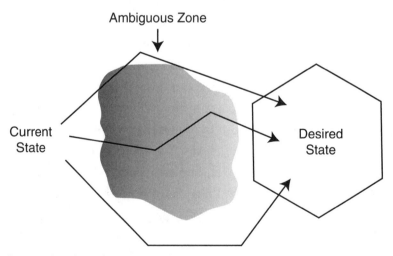

Figure 8-2   The Ambiguous Zone

[1] I've always called this the *ambiguous zone*, but a very good consultant and writer by the name of William Bridges has called it the *neutral zone*. I think it's more than neutral, since there is perceived danger there.

in their methodology. They look for results and output more than technology and input.

The wonderful, ironic comedian Steve Wright once observed that he would love to be able to daydream, but he keeps getting distracted! OOIs don't become distracted easily. They provide the guidance that helps their colleagues and their clients through the ambiguous zones of their careers and professional practices.

> *Stop It! Don't merely follow the crowd. We are not meant to be herd animals. You can often be fascinating to others merely by standing your ground as the crowd moves on.*

You've probably all seen sandpipers and plovers at the beach. They run along the shore to find small shellfish that the tides wash in, but they run like cartoon characters to escape from each breaking wave.

That constant running to and fro reminds me of many people in professional services such as coaching. They run toward food and opportunity, but retreat before their feet can get wet, constantly traveling with the flock.

But we're not in this business to stick our toe in the water, we're here to make waves. (At least, that's where a seven-figure income comes from, and the commensurate discretionary time that it generates.) You don't succeed in aggressive marketing if you're periodically retreating.

So an object of interest doesn't hop aboard for the social media platform follies, or utilize approaches to coaching picked up from mediocre coaches, or keep his or her head down while others are debating issues of the profession. You have to be somewhat bold and fearless and opinionated. You don't run from debate and merely quote the hackneyed gospels of the profession.

You punch holes and question smugness. You don't worry about initials after your name, but rather focus on clients on your résumé. You are on your way to thought leadership, not unqualified love.

If you want the latter, you can always get a dog.

THE MILLION DOLLAR CONSULTANT® ACCELERANT CURVE

I've organized and host a Million Dollar Club that meets annually in exotic locations around the world. We exchange insights, techniques, and intellectual capital. At our first meeting, a member named Mark Smith provided a simple and powerful comparison based on ease of doing business and fees. I dubbed this an "Accelerant Curve" and went about developing it for speakers, coaches, consultants, and related professions. See Figure 8-3.

The vertical axis represents decreasing barriers to entering into a relationship with you, and the horizontal represents increasing "intimacy" (personalized work with you) and higher fees. (Counterintuitively, this also represents *lower* labor intensity, as you'll discover in a few minutes.)

At number 1 on the vertical columns, you may provide free downloads on your site, or free podcasts. As you progress to number 4, you're offering booklets, manuals, books, low-priced teleconferences, and so on. Above, you'll see that these first four columns are "competitive," that is, not differentiated from others' offerings in any powerful way. They are means to allow people to get to know you and your value in an easy, inexpensive manner.

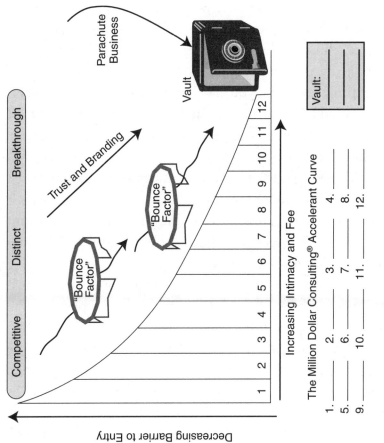

Figure 8-3 Million Dollar Consulting® Accelerant Curve

Columns 5 through 8, however, are labeled "distinctive." These are keynote speeches, one-day workshops, private remote coaching, one-day team-building efforts, audio/video coaching packages, and so on. People are working more closely with you in distinctive ways, at higher fees.

In columns 9 through 12, there are "breakthrough" offerings, which are uniquely yours. These are high intimacy and high fee. They may be extended coaching over several months, team coaching, sophisticated assessments, and so forth.

Finally, in your "vault" are personalized experiences that are entirely reliant on you and your relationship with a client. These would include long-term retainers, quarterly audits of personal and team progress, preparation of high performers for succession purposes, and so on.

Proceeding down the Accelerant Curve is a matter of trust and brand. The more you are trusted and the stronger your brand, the faster you will proceed. However, involvement with each column is intended to build that trust as well, enabling rapid progress down the curve.

I've discovered "bounce factors" that propel clients down the curve, skipping over many columns as they progress to the right. For example, many people who read my books (*Million Dollar Speaking, Million Dollar Consulting*, and the one you're now reading), which can be purchased for $15 to $30, will then "bounce down" to my Mentor Program ($3,500 to $14,000) or to one of my special events ($12,000 to $35,000). In my vault are offerings such as the Mentor Mastery Program, where I equip people to mentor others, and they obtain clients using my brand and the Accelerant Curve.

In addition, once the Accelerant Curve is functioning well, you'll acquire "parachute business," *which enters the chart on the right* through word of mouth and immediate trust.

The key is to have no "chasms," however. You can't afford to have people become interested at the upper left but have no easy "next steps" to develop a business relationship with you. Too many coaches have offerings on the extreme left and the extreme right, with nothing in between, and some have offerings solely in the middle, meaning that not only is it more difficult to get started with them, but, after starting, there's no place to go!

> *Stop It! You can't make seven figures in coaching with just a few service offerings at either end of the Accelerant Curve. You have to attract, nurture, and then retain clients who appreciate your value.*

I said that, counterintuitively, labor intensity *decreases* as you move to the right. How can that be if intimacy and personalization increase?

If you structure this correctly, you'll find that retainers and specialized interventions will rely on your quality and access to your smarts, not on your presence. Too many coaches seem to believe that their physical presence constitutes their value (and one swore to me that his audio program was his real value!). As we discussed in an earlier chapter, the "insurance policy" aspect of your being available for a key client, even by phone and e-mail and even once a month, has enormous impact.

Therefore, if you configure your right-hand offerings and your vault so that they are not labor-dependent but quality- and access-dependent, you'll achieve very high income with relatively little labor. As people have grown to trust you over the course of the accelerant trip—or if they've "parachuted in" because of strong trust and your strong brand—they will accept your formula for the best way in which to work together.

Don't mistake presence for value. This will kill you, and it's why you must charge for value (in this case, access) and never for time. (Retainers can have time durations, but you charge one fee regardless of how many times you are contacted.)

The columns on the curve are variable. You should be changing them as your experience and skills and value increase. Some will disappear and be replaced; others will move toward the right (e.g., your basic coaching fee increases from $15,000 to $25,000, or your retainer from $7,500 per month to $10,000). In fact, as your career matures and grows, the entire Accelerant Curve should shift to the right. Even at the easiest point of entry, in that case, people may be paying to engage you or obtain your products.

Replicate the chart in Figure 8-3 and spend some time determining how you can best fill it in at this point in your career, and what you have to plan and project to achieve that. The Accelerant Curve will make you a star once you attract people and help them to move rapidly to your unique value offerings.

THINK ABOUT BEING A THOUGHT LEADER

Thought leadership is one of these terms that's become worn out from use, yet, like *empowerment*, actually retains meaning and integrity. And it's very critical for coaches who wish to stand out in a crowd and build seven-figure practices.

A *thought leader* is someone who is actually a center of expertise, an object of interest, and a trailblazer. Thought leadership isn't loud, it's impressively soft. These people may march to the beat of that different drummer, but it's not necessarily a *louder* drummer. We're talking about creativity, not cacophony.

Here are the attributes of thought leadership:

- Is regularly cited by others, especially leaders in their fields.
- Has a peer group of similar, highly respected thinkers.
- Regularly introduces new intellectual property.
- Is sought out by the media, quoted, and interviewed.
- Has written commercially published books.
- Has a dramatic Web presence.
- Makes public appearances.
- Changes and evolves positions as justified by experiences.
- Will debate and defend positions.
- Has no fear of failure—not everything is correct or works.
- Is internationally known.
- Creates metaphors, analogies, and examples that are copied.
- Owns protected and proprietary works.
- In his or her niche, is virtually impossible not to know of.
- Has practical and immediately applicable ideas, not mere concepts.

At this writing, in professional services, here are some thought leaders of recent vintage (note that thought leadership can transcend one's death):

Coaching: Marshall Goldsmith
Innovation: Seth Godin

Investing: Warren Buffett
Leadership: John Gardner
Personal growth: Marcus Buckingham
Political strategy: Mary Matalin (and her husband, James
    Carville)
Professional speaking: Patricia Fripp
Sales: Jeff Gitomer
Small business development: David Maister
Societal trends: Malcolm Gladwell
Solo consulting: Alan Weiss
Strategic thinking: Peter Drucker
Technology: Walter Mossberg
Training and development: Robert Mager

There can obviously be more than one thought leader in any given niche or area. But the fact is that if you're in one of these areas and you have never heard of the appropriate name, then you're just fooling around—an amateur. You may not agree with the thought leader, and you may never have met him or her, but if you haven't heard of this person and don't know of his or her work in your own field, then you're simply not serious.

> *Stop It! Don't simply follow others' paths through the woods. Find your own, or buy a chopper and fly over the woods.*

If you seek to market aggressively—which this chapter aggressively suggests—then you should constantly strive to be considered a thought leader by those who are making buying decisions. The market gravity approach discussed in an earlier chapter is a great mechanism to ensure that your name, accomplishments, and intellectual property are constantly on view and accessible.

Thought leadership is refulgent. It creates both heat and light. The heat is the eagerness and urgency to learn and to grow, which attracts people to you. The light is the insight and techniques that you generate to lead those people.

As a coach (and probably, therefore, often as a consultant), find ways to develop and convey pragmatic new ideas.

- *Partner with your clients.* If you are involved with a novel new approach (coaching teams of clients and their customers together), seek permission to document and publicize the methodology and results. Your client may want to coauthor. If you can't get such permission, then capture the model and process and publicize it without revealing the client.

- *Exploit technology.* Everyone is in need of adaptations to be made for e-mail, Internet, i-Everything, and remote communications. What are you doing that makes you successful in this area, and how can you encapsulate and share it? What works for you will work for others.

- *Adopt a sharing mentality.* People ask why I "risk" my intellectual property by publishing it in so many books. The risk is in *not* publishing it and not being known or appreciated for my work! If you walk around fearing that people will steal from you and consequently hide your work and your insights, you'll have a very safe and very poor existence. You have to show people that you're a thought leader, not say, "If you could only see what I have locked up in the safe!"[2]

---

[2] I couldn't make this up: some bozo wanted me to coach him to market a dramatic "breakthrough" business process, but refused to divulge to me (or anyone else) what it was for fear of theft. I told him that he could pay me to coach him, but I wouldn't reveal my coaching methods, so he would have to assume that he was being coached.

- *Recombine.* There is little new under the sun (the pharaohs had need of coaches to build the pyramids, but they employed more primitive motivation techniques), but if you can adjust and merge existing ideas to reflect the contemporary mores, economics, and technology, you'll always be ahead of the game. The iPhone and iPad are huge recombinations of existing technologies, just as global coaching can combine remote needs with language skills, cultural realities, and career planning.

If you seek to build a million dollar coaching practice, it's de rigueur to become a thought leader, because that position generates publicity, so that people come to you and fees are not an issue; it enables retainer work, so that labor intensity is lowered and discretionary time (real wealth) is maximized; and it provides for media attention, which is viral and a natural competitive advantage over the people who are following your lead.

But you can do still more to leverage your thought leadership. Read on, and learn how to play and listen to the music.

BLOWING YOUR OWN HORN (OR LIVING WITHOUT MUSIC)

I mentioned earlier that thought leadership was about a different drummer, but not necessarily a louder drummer. However, there has to be percussion. There has to be sound. You can't be the tree falling in the deserted forest.

If you don't blow your own horn, there is no music.

One of the fundamental problems with low self-esteem is the belief (and commensurate manifestations) that you're not deserving, don't merit attention, and can't justify your true value. This makes it virtually impossible for you to promote yourself, however rationally and professionally. There are also backgrounds and former professions that create a "low-profile norm": therapy, teaching, accounting, law, design, midlevel management, and so forth.

Great coaches cannot be mendicants. They can't be obsequious or sycophantic. Early in his career, Marshall Goldsmith managed to gain board membership at the Peter Drucker Foundation in the mid-1960s, where he coedited his first book. If you met Mr. Goldsmith, your impression would probably not be of a shy, retiring professor (although he once was one). He's dynamic, opinionated, and assertive, and there's not much doubt that he can help you (or anyone else, for that matter).

If you review my list of thought leaders in the prior section, you're not going to find one of them who is terribly reluctant to tell you why he's right and how he can help you!

Rest easy, I'm not talking about creating television infomercials with all those happy (paid) audience participants screaming for a new juicer for $19.95 ("But wait, order now and . . ."). Nor am I suggesting the deadly direct mail and "cold calls" of the slicksters who have never really done anything of substance but send direct mail, spam, and make cold calls. (There is a famous "coach" who founded a coaching magazine and promptly had herself named "coach of the year" or something! I'm not sure whether a juicer came along with the honor.)

Here are mechanisms by which and through which you can blow your own horn in good taste, in tune, on pitch, but as a solo recital.

Use "Parachute Stories"

When you are speaking or publishing, use your own experiences. You can hide the client's name, but indicate your personal role in the success. For example, instead of saying, "The use of 360-degree feedback with customers can provide additional insights," say, "When I pioneered the use of 360-degree feedback with investors at a major securities firm, we created an entirely new dimension in assessing management performance."

You need to connect yourself to the outcomes and results, not merely cite them as if you're remarking on an inexorable natural phenomenon. What did you do, how did you do it, and what was the impact?

Use Power Language

People are moved by action and assertiveness, not by observation and passivity. Don't use the passive voice if you can help it. Instead of saying, "We were fortunate to have conditions that allowed us to . . .," say, "We recognized a unique opportunity and created a unique feedback system that . . ."

This chapter is about aggressive marketing and becoming a star. You do that with power and direction, demonstrating that you don't merely respond to requests but actually create dramatic and innovative change.

Focus on Emotional Impact

Logic makes people think, but emotion makes them act. Behind every corporate objective is a personal objective. Find out what's important to the individual—legacy, discretionary time, less stress, applying more talents—and highlight those personal benefits as well.

Don't allow yourself to "merely" focus on grand organizational improvement. Include the immediacy of personal needs met and short-term gratification.

> *Stop It! Don't sell yourself short in word or deed.
> If the first sale is to yourself, make it a substantial
> transaction!*

Emphasize Innovative Work, Not Merely Problem Solving

There is nothing exciting or compelling about remedial action. There is something that stirs the blood, however, about raising performance to new heights, outstripping the competition, breaking new ground—you get the idea.

What are you doing to demonstrate "the best getting better," being the "all-star coach," or "setting new standards"? There is far too much coaching focused on improving the laggards until they become average, and far too little on investing in the best so that they invigorate results even more.

Audit Your Collateral and Your Web Site

Your print and electronic materials should reflect a star presence, not another humdrum billboard along the roadside or extended résumé. At a *minimum*, here is what to look for, improve, and/or create:

- *Video testimonials.* Have those clients who are willing provide a 30-second endorsement of your methods and results. (This is sometimes easier when the buyer is not the client.) In hard copy, have these on letterhead in a "testimonial book" that is bound and shows plaudits over time.[3]

---

[3] This is where a "prior life" can often get in your way. Shake off the belief that coaching clients won't provide endorsements, or that it's somehow "inappropriate" to ask for them. I will guarantee this: you won't get any if you don't ask for them.

- *Typical client results.* Do *not* focus on your methodology or credentials. Focus on "what's in it for the client." Create a dynamic, dramatic list of what clients can reasonably expect from working with you, based on your experience and your talents.

- *Case studies.* Provide examples (these can be amalgams, and you needn't use specifics) of how you specifically help clients. I recommend three brief paragraphs: situation, intervention, resolution. Cite the situation you encountered (quick demand for media skills), your course of action (assembled a pseudo-press corps), and the outcome (smoothly handles extemporaneous questions under pressure). Allow people to identify with what you've done for others.

Create Public Stimulation and Comment

Create 5- to 10-minute podcasts (which can go on iTunes, for example), 10-minute videos (which can go on YouTube), blog posts, and other media interventions that allow you to extend your intellectual property and encourage others to comment on it. Use Google Alerts, which is free, for key phrases and your name, to find out where you're being mentioned, repeated, and cited.

These are inexpensive alternatives that you can produce at any time and with a frequency that will keep your horn playing above the fray and noise. If you don't do that, your audience will be hearing someone else's tune.

But if you do it well, you can soon have your own orchestra.

DEVELOPING YOURSELF

THE ÜBER-COACH

THE SKI INSTRUCTOR NEEDS TO BE IN FRONT OF YOU

Skiing is a wonderful family sport, and when we all took it up, I quickly learned about the cult of skiing, the lodge, après ski, and so on. Nonetheless, I haven't engaged in many sports where, by the time you get to the starting line (the top of the hill), you're already exhausted (don the equipment, get the tickets, get on the line, ride the lift, prepare for the descent . . .).

There is a lot of advice circulating in ski venues, a quotidian condition. But some of it is provided by people in exquisite ski outfits, adorned with furs and various animal parts, sitting by the fire, holding a glass of brandy, and expounding on the best form of traverse. Like about 90 percent of the boats at the marina near my home, these people never actually move.

The ski instructor I hired checked out my equipment with me, went up the hill sitting next to me, and then skied down it in front of me with his posterior about six yards ahead of my skis, doing what I should be doing, and occasionally looking back to make sure I was still on my feet.

Now THAT was a coach.

I relate this at some length because, ironically, as you become successful, you are in ever greater danger of the success trap. You need to find better and better people to use as avatars, to seek as coaches for yourself, and to emulate. As you go up the hill to tougher and tougher trails, there are, naturally, fewer and fewer outstanding skiers, and even fewer of them who can coach others.

The term "coaching" at this writing gets 61 million hits on Google. "Top management coaches" narrows it to 35 million. And here's the kicker: "coaching universities" generates more than 7 million responses!

As you get better, how do you become great? Here are some criteria to use, because you have to be prepared for success. Too many people wrap themselves around the prevention of failure. But outstanding people are constantly preparing to exploit and capitalize on success.

Find Someone Who Has Done What You Want to Do, Repeatedly

There is a plethora of "flashes in the pan," one-book wonders, who were lucky and decided that luck was actually talent. A lot of people can publish a book, close a consulting contract, or get a speaking assignment. (Just look around and think about some of the absolute schlock you've seen.) But *very few* can do that consistently.

If someone has coached within major organizations for a decade, has a very high-profile list of clients, has written four books on the subject, or is constantly cited in the media, there's a good chance that this person has the expertise to help you. However, see the next point.

Find Someone with the Ability and Volition to Help You

Not everyone who can coach can teach other coaches. We've all observed terrific managers, athletes, and professionals who can't seem to develop a successor, or expand their expertise to the team, or tutor colleagues. These are people who either can't or won't articulate their processes for high performance.

Thus, the person who has the capabilities and the track record (which is the content) must also have the communications skills and motivation to convey what's needed (which is the process). Not surprisingly, you have to be more careful in choosing your own coach than your average client!

In Figure 9-1, you can see that the charlatan has no content and no ability to transfer skills, but is just trying to take

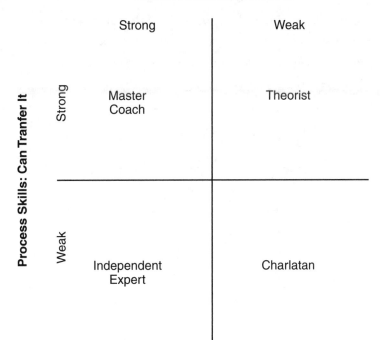

Figure 9-1 Content and Process Expertise

your money. The independent expert is smart and successful, but is unable to transfer skills. The theorist can advise you all day long, but has never really done what is being preached. (I suspect this includes every university professor of education in the country.)

Only the master coach has the ability to coach other coaches: an indisputable track record of success and the wherewithal to convey key principles, techniques, and methodologies to others. That's worth paying for, and you're seldom going to find it in a class of 25 others, or a "program" with an inflexible regimen or an arbitrary time period.

At this level of success, your own development should be customized and tailored for your particular needs: your talents, marketplace, history, practice characteristics, likely future, personal objectives, and so on.

> *Stop It! Don't feel obligated to listen to unsolicited feedback, even from your peers. Find people whom you trust based on their success, and solicit the feedback that you require.*

Constantly Stretch Yourself

When I was struggling to make it in this profession, I developed an interesting verbal tic: whenever buyers asked if I could do something for them, I said, "Of course." I found that I could scramble and seek and search, and I'd figure out how to do something, which was far better than responding, "Well, I've never done that before and I'll have to create my learning curve, and get some help, and you'd be the laboratory . . ."

Believe in yourself, find the help you need offline and situationally as required, and remember that you are the best one to help this client. Thus, pursue business and projects that are out-

> ### Digression
>
> *Once I was asked by Merck to design training and coaching around Criterion Referenced Instruction (CRI), which at the time was a "must" for such work within Merck. My buyer said, "I assume you can get up to speed, so get us a proposal to start in two weeks. If that's a problem, tell me."*
>
> *I wasn't about to make it a problem. I called the CRI guru, Robert Mager, who lived in Carefree, Arizona. "How long would it take to train me?" I asked. "It's a 17-day process," he said. "I don't have 17 days," I explained. "How long do you have?" he inquired. "A couple of days at most," I calculated. "Come out this weekend," he said, and over two days he taught me everything I needed to know about CRI and how to drink a perfect Manhattan.*

side your comfort zone and in places where you've never worked, and by all means *never* turn away business, because you can help the client. If you have that mental set, will it work for you?

Of course.

CREDENTIALS DON'T MATTER; A TRACK RECORD OF SUCCESS DOES

I've belonged to several organizations where a third of the members had "MA" after their names. I honestly thought that it was a fluke that so many of them were from Massachusetts.

Then I learned that the initials signified "master of arts," and I have *never* seen that degree used after someone's name in any other milieu. I have seen MBA, even MSW (master of social work), but this was a desperate attempt to engage in the bizarre ritual of ACBAI (adding credibility by adding initials).

I can string 17 initials after my name: Ph.D., CMC (Certified Management Consultant), FIMC (Fellow of the Institute of Management Consultants), CSP (Certified Speaking Professional), CPAE (Council of Peers Award for Excellence in professional speaking)—and I'm probably forgetting a few. Meanwhile, my business card says just "Alan Weiss," and I use Ph.D. to make dinner reservations and doctors' appointments. ("Dr. Weiss? Of course we'll fit you in.")

Coaches today can acquire ICF, LCC, PCC, MCC, CEC, and so on—an alphabet of certifications, memberships, and strange relationships. There are people who will tell you that "credentialing" is the credibility statement of the future. The problem is that they are empirically wrong. There are so many of these loony honorifics today that everyone with a brain is skeptical.

Basically, *if the buyer doesn't recognize the credential, it's worthless.* No one in over 30 years has ever asked me about "official" credentials, and only one person—the CEO of Merck at the time, Roy Vagelos—has ever bothered to ask what school I attended (Rutgers).

What does matter is a track record, and those are easier to assemble than you might think. At this stage of your career, moving to the top of the profession, you should have established a brand or brands. The ultimate brand is your name ("Get me Jane Murphy"), but you can develop any number of brands.

As you can see in Figure 9-2, your brand is "magic" when market needs (which you can create and anticipate), your competency, and your passion meet in a powerful confluence. If you have passion and market need, but no competency, you'll lose to the competition; if you have passion and competency, but no market need, you have a message that no one wants to hear; and

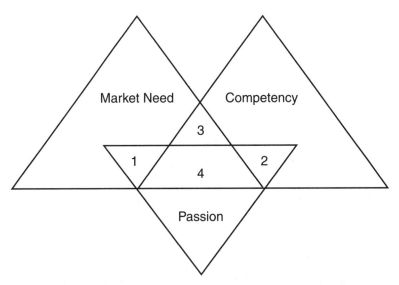

1. Brand is a clever concept, but substance can't be delivered.
2. Brand is ideally suited to you, but market is unreceptive.
3. Brand is potentially effective, but isn't supported.
4. Brand is magic.

Figure 9-2   Market Effectiveness Factor

if you have market need and competency, but no passion, you have a nine-to-five job!

> *Stop It! Never sit back and rely on past success or traditional sources of business. Build a track record and brand so that new clients are constantly attracted to you.*

Brand fits with market gravity as shown in Figure 9-3, using the three factors from Figure 9-2.

Whether you're new to the profession or a veteran, you should examine the power of your brand. But in becoming a super coach, those are imperatives.

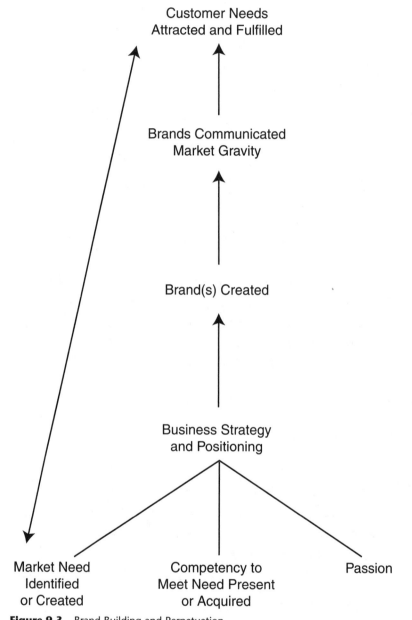

Figure 9-3   Brand Building and Perpetuation

You build your track record and manifest its power in these ways:

Gather testimonials. Ask every client for testimonials. In coaching, there is a chance that the client will demur, but especially when the buyer and client are different, the buyer may be in a position to provide you with print and video endorsements.

Use a client list. Unless this is expressly forbidden by the client organization, you can list a business as a client. Over the years, this list should become impressive.

Achieve stature in the profession. We'll cover this further later in the chapter when we discuss intellectual property and trademarks, but play a role in the profession itself, at events, in publications, and in interviews. Instead of gathering initials, provide innovation.

Create models and approaches from experience. You should seldom be "surprised" at this point in your career, and virtually anything you're presented with you should have been involved with before. (I've claimed that there are only 11 issues in all of organizational development work!)

On your Web site, in your blog, in your newsletters, in your speeches, and in your conversations, don't focus on your credentials, focus on your track record of improving individuals, teams, and client organizations. Develop and manifest your brands wherever possible, and make sure that your name is attached to your work.

As you develop yourself into the über-coach, your mindset must be that you have significant value to share to improve others, and that it's incumbent upon you to allow others to appreciate that value. And every year that value should be increasing by dint of your experience, repute, and self-development activities. Remember the Accelerant Curve: you want to constantly move clients toward your personal "vault."

Let's take a look at that combination.

MOVING INTO CONSULTING, SPEAKING, PUBLISHING, AND OTHER AREAS

One technique that will really open up the Accelerant Curve and leave you firmly situated at the right is to diversify your delivery options. We aren't a label on our business cards, after all. We are sources of help, of intellectual capital, of value—and the more options we provide for people to access that value, the more benefit we can provide to more people.

That's the mindset that I referred to earlier: we are here to help others, and it is, therefore, incumbent upon us to

1. Let them know that we are here (blow your own horn).
2. Create attraction (marketing gravity).
3. Manifest value (object of interest).
4. Create more intimate and profitable relationships (Accelerant Curve).
5. Achieve acclaim (thought leadership and branding).
6. Broaden our appeal (diversify our offerings).

While you needn't follow that sequence in strict order, it is a rational progression. You attract attention, draw people to you, fascinate them, develop long-term relationships, become a niche leader, and then broaden the niche.

Too many people seem to jump directly to point 6 or forget to engage in point 3, and so on. At this point in this book, and at some point in your career (perhaps now?), you're truly ready for point 6.

Speaking[1]

Earlier I advocated speaking for marketing purposes, an important point in the market gravity discipline. But now I'm talking about speaking professionally. As a coach, you've learned a great deal about

- Conflict resolution
- Negotiating
- Problem solving and decision making
- Leadership styles
- Organizational dynamics
- Dealing with promotions
- Providing feedback

The list goes on. These are ideal speaking topics for any number of trade association and private organization meetings.

If you're comfortable speaking to groups and/or have learned these skills while marketing, start with trade associations, which often place a room full of buyers and recommenders in front of speakers. A key resource is *National Trade and Professional Associations of the United States* (there are similar works for other countries), which is available in hard copy and online (https://www.columbiabooks.com) and provides the

---

[1] For detailed descriptions of these pursuits, see my books *Million Dollar Consulting*, 4th ed. (New York: McGraw-Hill, 2009) and *Million Dollar Speaking* (New York: McGraw-Hill, 2010), and the Appendix.

name of the association and its executive director, budget, membership, conference dates, and other such information for more than 10,000 organizations. (At this writing, if you use my name, you will get a 20 percent discount—I have no financial relationship with the publisher; that is simply a benefit that I can provide for you.)

Consulting

You actually *are* consulting when you coach. Consultants are people who improve the client's condition. They do so through skills, experiences, and knowledge, and they correct and/or elevate the client's organizational performance and individual performance. This may take the form of audits, training, observation, redesign, strategic direction, tactical advice, retainers, and so on. Clearly, coaching is a subset. *Most consultants are already coaching in one form or another*, since you can't improve people or advise management without coaching them (which is why I detest and mock the artificial lines drawn between coaching and consulting).

To become adept at consulting, you merely need to move up the food chain a few steps. After all, you can advise management on

- Interpersonal relations
- Incentives
- Evaluations
- Communications
- Morale
- Environment
- Effective listening

You get the idea. Take the knowledge and skills that you've developed and apply them to systems, procedures, surroundings, and very large groups. Incorporate your coaching into the consulting assignment. If this is appealing and you've never done it, try my book *Getting Started in Consulting*, 3rd ed. (Newark, N.J.: John Wiley & Sons, 2009).

Consulting will open up the right-hand side of the Accelerant Curve, will create much higher fee levels, and is a very natural progression from your coaching activities. Don't allow someone's arbitrary boundary line to artificially delimit your career. That roundelay needs to be stopped. I've been consulting since 1985 and coaching since 1985.

> *Stop It! Don't allow a label to set boundaries on your career. Define yourself by your outputs and results, not your tasks and titles.*

Publishing

It may be time for you to consider commercial publishing, which will dramatically spread your message and can strongly contribute to your income all along the Accelerant Curve. It's not about how many books you sell, by the way; it's about getting them into the right hands. My worst-selling book of 40 was my strategy book (now known as *Best Laid Plans*, originally *Making It Work* from HarperCollins). But I "made" about $2.5 million from the strategy work it generated.

If you review the thought leaders of an earlier chapter, you'll find that all of us are authors, some of us multiple times. My books are in nine languages, and I've been to 59 countries. Those are not independent events.

Here's a quick authorship guide:

I. Why Write a Book?

   A. It is the second-best credibility source (IF commercially published).[2]

   B. It establishes a brand with great effectiveness.

   C. It creates a "downslope" for continuous publishing (momentum).

   D. It forces you to connect and configure your own methodology.

   E. It is an outstanding source of passive income.

   F. It helps your ego and provides fulfillment.

   G. It allows for ongoing learning (understanding what you don't know).

II. How to Write a Book

   A. First have something to say, or don't read on.

   B. Think of the reader and the audience, not yourself.

   C. Don't just whine—offer solutions and hope.

   D. Focus on the pragmatic, not the esoteric.

   E. Use memorable language, phrases, and metaphors.

   F. Do not try to copy others' success (*Chicken Soup for the Turkeys*).

   G. Discipline, structure, and planning:

- Create calendar time.
- Create contingency time.
- Be undisturbed and unmolested, but above all comfortable.
- Use a framework (X chapter, Y pages, Z written per day).
- Use variants (mini-interviews, case studies).

---

[2] First-best is peer-to-peer reference.

H. Don't write everything you know; *write what the reader needs to know.*

I. Attribute meticulously, but don't borrow too much.

J. Write conversationally.

III. How to Commercially Publish a Book

A. Create a treatment/proposal. This should include

- Theme (title and purpose)
- Table of contents
- One chapter in its entirety (any chapter, 20+ pages)
- Two paragraphs about all other chapters
- A half-page on your unique credentials
- Several pages on a competitive marketing analysis
- Description of the primary, secondary, and tertiary audiences
- Description of the unique marketing assets you bring
- Distinctions of the book (e.g., interviews, self-tests, and so on)
- Estimated length and delivery time

B. Choose an agent or acquisition editor by name.

C. Write a cover letter and submit the treatment.

- Multiple submissions are fine.

D. Don't jump at a contract.

- If you have no agent, use a good lawyer (not your cousin Louie).

E. Understand that you will have to promote.

F. Beware of advice from others.

- One book is an accident, two are a coincidence, three are a pattern.
- Remember the ski instructor!

There are other elements that you may wish to consider in your diversification: products (audio, video, text, and/or combinations), teleconferences, Webinars, workshops, training other coaches (we'll discuss this later in the chapter), and self-published books, checklists, manuals, workbooks, and so on. Before too long, maybe by the time you read this, I plan to have my own "apps" for the iPhone!

Once you begin to develop this amount of "stuff" (as George Carlin would say), it's also time to consider protecting it.

CREATING UNIQUE INTELLECTUAL PROPERTY AND TRADEMARKS

Once you've gained a certain stature and reputation, and your intellectual property is flowing over the landscape, it's vital that you protect your assets without becoming paranoid. Here are some guidelines that are often ignored by or unknown to coaches, since they tend to rely ordinarily on strictly interpersonal actions. But at this stage of your career, your intellectual property becomes crucial to lower labor intensity and creating passive income.

Don't forget, wealth is discretionary time.

Copyrights

Once you put something in written form, it's automatically copyrighted, so long as it's your original material. You can place the traditional © mark or "Copyright Tom Smith" and include "2011, all rights reserved," if you like. (Many trademark and patent attorneys, but not all, recommend "© Tom Smith, 2011. All rights reserved." You never use © and "copyright" together.)[3]

You can file your material with the U.S. (or another nation's) Copyright Office, but you needn't, and doing so can be VERY time consuming once you consider the sheer volume of material that you create. The only benefit in doing so is this: in a copyright dispute, you can sue to prevent someone else from illegally using your copyrighted material. However, you cannot collect punitive damages unless you have registered with the government. I've never sought to do that over 30 years.

Note that you cannot copyright or otherwise protect a book title or a speech that's simply delivered orally, under most conditions.

You cannot use others' copyrighted material without permission, except for brief excerpts for citation and/or reviews, and you must always attribute the source. I've actually had to deal with people who copied huge parts of my and several others' materials, then "recombined them in a unique way," according to the violator, and created a "new" work. We put a stop to that.

Trademarks and Service Marks and Registration

You can trademark (^{TM}) and service mark (^{SM}) your property, depending on the nature of the use (e.g., a phrase, workshop, descriptive words, models, graphics, and so on). If they are ulti-

---

[3] Obviously, consult your own attorney; this isn't meant to be legal advice, although I do play a lawyer on television.

mately unchallenged, they will receive registration (®), which is the highest form of protection. You file with the Commissioner of Patents and Trademarks.

Essentially, you are trying to claim "prior usage" and that the property originated with you *in your particular category*. For example, my partner, Patricia Fripp, and I have an LLC called The Odd Couple®, and we conduct seminars and run a community for professional speakers under that name. Despite the prior use of this phrase as a theatrical event (play and movie), our category is radically different: developmental workshops and seminars. Hence (and to our surprise), we were able not just to use it, but to protect it, and we've since stopped two others from using the name for their workshops, since it is a brand that we've created.

Some "authorities" will advise you to use the Internet to conduct trademark searches and file the appropriate papers yourself, for about $250 or so. I advise you never to do that, because your property is too important for you try to be your own lawyer (would you advise someone to be his or her own coach?). Get a good trademark attorney (this is a specialty in the law), and expect to pay between $600 and $800. The search will be more comprehensive, someone else will do the filing more efficiently, and the expert will know how to follow up. And you'll save $10,000 of your time and have a greater chance of success.

Generic words are tough to protect. I can't protect Million Dollar Consulting, but I can protect its use as an adjective: Million Dollar Consulting® College. It usually takes six to nine months for the trademark to become registered, but that can be complicated if someone else claims prior use or if the trademark office finds your request too vague or too similar to others. *However, you can begin using the ™ mark immediately upon filing.*

> *Stop It! Million Dollar Coaches express their value in far more diverse ways than solely one-on-one coaching, and the key to doing so is to create and protect the intellectual capital that you translate into salable intellectual property. That will become increasingly important as your career matures.*

Consistent Use and Extra Protection

If a usage becomes dormant over many years, others may step in and try to claim it. Copyright and trademark protections don't last forever and often must be renewed, still more reasons why you need a good attorney.

However, you can do even more to protect yourself without being paranoid. For example:

- Use a device such as Google Search, which is free. You can create your own terms and phrases, and you'll be told every day where they are being cited and used on the Internet. Thus, I can find my name, Million Dollar Consulting, Value Based Fees, and so on quite readily. This tells me who is helping me and who may be ripping me off. (You'll also learn about your competition if you put in their trademarked phrases and names.)
- Sites such as Copyscape (http://www.copyscape.com) allow you to insert a URL (for example, of one of your Web pages or online articles) and see where else it is appearing. I found a woman who had lifted five complete pages from my site to use as her own! I found another man who had virtually copied my site and property. We easily stopped this legally, and my

lawyer claimed that it was the worst, dumbest case of plagiarism he had ever seen.

- When you speak, also use a handout with your key points and models and the appropriate trademarks, service marks, and copyrights in writing. (If you tell a story when you speak, it is not protected if it's not written down, and there is a huge amount of such theft in the speaking profession.)

- Use your name whenever possible, which will also build your brand as a by-product. Instead of "Ten Tips to Better Influence," call it "Jane Peters's Ten Tips to Better Influence."

- Place your copyright notice on *every page*, because pages often become separated and/or are independently copied.

Nothing will ever take the place of the dynamic, interactive, highly skilled individual. However, you *do* often want your intellectual property to either market that potential or follow up with additional revenue. It's atavistic to believe that people will always respect your property and honor the source. With the Web, advertent and inadvertent theft has become viral.

You can't prevent it, but you can discourage it. As when your house has a burglar alarm and a large dog, the chances are that you've reduced your chances of a break-in.

COACHING OTHER COACHES: LICENSING

Let's conclude this chapter on becoming the über-coach by examining what would be required to become a coach's coach.

This would not be an arbitrary training period followed by a framed diploma, but rather an experiential opportunity that utilizes your experience, skills, intellectual property, and passion. This is a "vault" item on the Accelerant Curve.

Moreover, this is a very critical way to increase passive income while concurrently building your brand. In this profession, there are only two business models, both of which can be highly successful.

Building a Company

In this model, you build a firm, with employees, assets, infrastructure, goodwill, and so forth. As you grow, you reinvest in the firm, so that you are limited in what you can extract personally each year. Any benefit plans that you install for yourself and your dependents must also apply to all employees and their dependents. The intent is that in some reasonable time frame— 10 to 20 years—you will sell the enterprise for tens of millions of dollars and pursue a second career or just relax. Many people have done exactly that.

The problems include

- Limited ability to create personal wealth early
- Disposition to manage people needed
- More complex legal and accounting issues
- More threat (theft of clients, theft of intellectual property)
- Firm never gains a high enough valuation to justify sale
- The brand must be with the firm, not with you, or the sale will require your continued participation under new ownership in some capacity

Building a Solo Practice

This is my model and the approach espoused in this book. It requires that you operate lean and mean, without staff, utilizing subcontractors and independents for your basic needs (graphic design, audiovisual, Web, and so forth) and for your business support (subcontractors, alliance partners). The intent is to maximize both your annual income and your discretionary time, and to build enough wealth so that you can eventually pursue other options or simply relax. The company name is merely a legal framework, with no inherent sales value or equity.

The problems include

- It's tough if you have high affiliation needs—it's lonely.
- There is no ready backup if you're sick or incapacitated.
- The brand must be your name, and market gravity is essential.
- Clients can be skeptical of "lone wolf" operations.
- You are dependent on "unsupervised" independent parties.
- You can't depend on safety nets.

The key for the practitioner—you—is to choose one of these models and not be straddling them, because they move apart as careers mature, and if you have one foot on each ledge, you'll have a growing chasm beneath you. Speakers who have "a couple of employees" who are doing things like making outgoing calls, handling "administration," or "running the office" either are lousy time managers or have to have their ego bolstered by claiming that they have "employees." You don't need them in a solo practice. Even the ubiquitous "virtual assistants" are a waste of time and money in an era of cell phones and e-mail.[4]

There is a great "loophole" or saving grace for the solo practitioner, however, that compensates for not having a firm to sell somewhere down the road. Where there might have been a lacuna, there is instead a diamond mine.

You can sell your intellectual property *divorced from your participation*. This is why developing intellectual property is so vital as your career progresses. You can license it to clients or to other coaches.

> *Stop It! Your value is not solely in your physical presence (if mine were, you wouldn't be reading this book). Your value can be extended through intellectual property, but that means that you have to stop viewing value as being equivalent to your direct involvement.*

When you license to clients, you provide your coaching tools and approaches to internal client coaches. That would usually involve

- Selecting and vetting potential coaches
- Formal training in classrooms
- "Apprenticeship" work as they observe you
- Evaluation work as you observe them
- Written material and job aids
- Access to you as needed for tough problems

---

[4] I've had to dissuade people making $150,000 a year from paying an assistant $30,000 of it.

- Periodic quality checks
- Involvement in larger communities of peers that you create

In organizations with large groups of salespeople, customer call center agents, retail representatives, or support staff, this kind of internal coaching is cost-effective for the client and lucrative for you. Your licensing fees will depend on the size of the organization and the number of coaches prepared, but they could easily be in six figures for the first year and $25,000 or more "maintenance" in successive years.

In licensing to other coaches, you can create global programs in which your experiences and techniques (and even your brand) are utilized to help others to gain more acceleration in their careers and embrace best practices more quickly. If you think of the niche leaders cited in an earlier chapter, acolytes love to gather to learn in their leader's real or virtual presence. Once you arrive at the top of your field in terms of your brand, thought leadership, and intellectual property—that is, once people readily point to you as an avatar of success in the profession—you can enrich other professionals' lives. Your options can embrace

- Master coaching sessions (envision a performer's "master class")
- Manuals, workbooks, and job aids
- Mentoring by phone and e-mail
- Periodic "state-of-the-art" conferences or symposia
- Workshops and seminars
- Differentiated proficiency levels and support
- Creation of peer-level, interactive communities

- Newsletters, teleconferences, videos, and podcasts
- Private Web sites and chat rooms

You get the idea. Earlier, I raised the question relative to the "coaching universities" about "who certifies the certifiers?" At this stage of your career, you now know the answer.

You do.

HIGHER LEVELS

REALLY, WHAT'S
THE POINT?

WEALTH IS DISCRETIONARY TIME

We're going to end this book with a discussion of the real purpose of the preceding nine chapters: why arrive at this station?

First, let's establish that stations and terminals are two different entities. A station is a stop along the way. The terminal is
the end of the line. I'm not talking about terminals; I'm talking
about the next station, since neither you nor I can be certain
about what awaits each of us, or when, at the end of the line.

Second, this is all about mindset. Your beliefs, values, and
perceptions will inform your behaviors. The sequence looks
like this (for your clients, as well):

Beliefs   Influenced by enlightened self-interest
Attitudes   Influenced by norms and mores
Behavior   Influenced by coercion and rules

Too often, behaviors are simply dealt with through carrots
and sticks, without any examination of the roots of the behav-

ior. Attitudes are often affected by "in-crowd" norms (no one is as conformist as the conventionally nonconformist) or by organizational appeal (don't be the only one to stop us from 100 percent participation in the blood drive).

The most effective and committed (as opposed to compliant) method of changing behavior—both others' and *yours*—is through appeals to enlightened self-interest. I use the term *enlightened* to indicate interest that is not met through unethical or illegal means or at the inappropriate expense of others.

So when I suggest to you that real wealth is discretionary time, I believe that, and it informs my attitudes and behaviors. I will not cancel, compromise, or reschedule a vacation for a client demand. On the other hand, I don't mind returning calls from the beach or checking e-mail twice a day from a resort. The critical element is realizing that you don't—DO NOT—have a personal life and a professional life; you simply have *a life*.

Consequently, how you choose to use that life is the most important set of decisions that you will have to constantly make and adjust. This is not a recondite or arcane pursuit. You can always make another dollar, but you can't make another minute.

The excuse that "there is no time" is as specious emanating from you as it is coming from a client. Every day has 24 hours at every stage of our careers and our lives. The question, therefore, becomes one of how you intend to use those hours, meaning that the more discretion you have, the wealthier you actually are. You can work so hard making the fuel, money, that you lose that discretion.

Some people work so hard making money that they destroy their wealth.

To behave in that manner, your beliefs have to stimulate your attitudes and actions. Tactically, that means that you must adapt habits such as

- Not being interrupted at the whim of others, meaning that your cell phone is useful for time-shifting and returning calls, not for being disturbed at arbitrary times
- Shifting appropriate work to the client, including scheduling, gathering information, and meetings
- Utilizing remote devices when they are qualitatively effective, and not "showing up" just because you're asked
- Embracing value-based fees and understanding that your *time* is not of value to the client, but that the *results* are

Strategically, you must understand that your career progression should have an impact on how you do business. To quote Marshall Goldsmith's dictum, "What got you here won't get you there." Figure 10-1 gives an illustration.

As your career progresses, you should be reaching out to prospects far less, and they should be seeking you out far more. That means that your mechanisms for attracting them (the market gravity that we've discussed) should increase in number, frequency, diversity, and effectiveness. You should move more and more out of your prior comfort zones in your efforts to attract people.

Commensurately, you must wean yourself away from the labor-intensive methods of reaching out with low success rates, such as cold calls, direct mail, networking, and so forth. These have to be overt and explicit changes fostered by your belief system. And this can be tricky.

I run a Million Dollar Club that meets once a year in exotic locations. Every member is earning seven figures in consulting, coaching, and related professional services. At our very first meeting, we were astonished to find that every single one

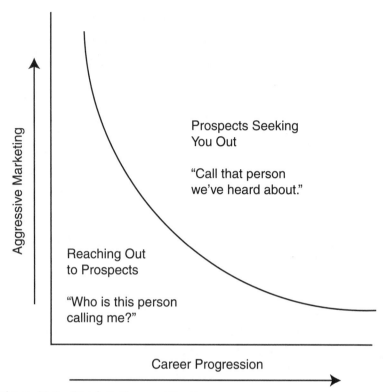

Figure 10-1   "Reach Out" versus Attraction

of us was engaged in some activities that we were no longer pas-sionate about, that weren't as profitable as they once were, *and that could not possibly generate sufficient business to take us to our next level and/or next set of life goals.*

This is a version of the "success trap" that I discussed ear-lier. We keep doing things that we're already good at, which is a serious error for successful people, and one that we'll discuss at length in the next segment.

Finally, a crucial element that even veteran coaches tend to forget, ignore, or do poorly is to create and nurture brands. As I've mentioned, the ultimate brand is your name ("Get me Harry Anderson"). But interim brands help, and many of them can happily coexist with your name or serve under that "umbrella." I'm still referred to at times as "the Contrarian," which was my very first brand, and my blog's URL address is contrarianconsulting.com. Whether you are new to the profession or a veteran, you should continually

- Create, evaluate, and promote new brands while discarding unsuccessful or outdated ones.
- Promote and develop your name as a brand (e.g., Jennifer West's Best Practices for Sales Coaches).

Figure 10-2 shows one way to view the development and "recycling" of brand value.

In Figure 10-2, your assets and your current services and products are tested against likely customers (clients and buyers), considering the economy and the competition. You use the crucible of your actual successes to focus on the most powerful

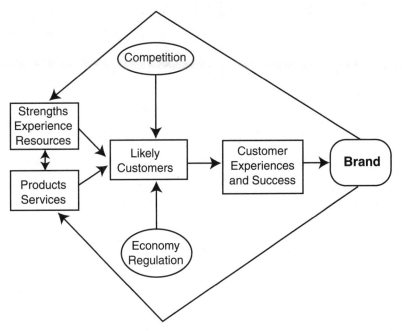

Figure 10-2   Brand Renewal

brand statements, which then flow back to improve your strengths, experiences, and resources (assets) and increase your products and services in terms of more and more appealing offerings (because your brand will create value to the point where you can inform people about what they need and not just respond to what they claim they want).

World-class coaching is about engaging in a constant, but rewarding and balanced climb. Let's look at the terrain.

IT'S NOT GOOD ENOUGH TO BE BETTER AT WHAT'S ALREADY GOOD

The major obstacle that confronts professional services providers in reaching initial success is a lack of self-esteem, which we've discussed earlier. Lack of belief in one's worth and value undermines one's efforts to establish credibility with others.

Once that is overcome, the greatest obstacle in trying to reach new levels of success is the "success trap," that is, continuing to improve what you're already very good at doing. The reasons for this second obstacle, which is the great barrier to higher levels of achievement, include

- *Safety.* You've taken risks, established success, and achieved a lifestyle that makes future risk taking seem far, far more intimidating. It's one thing to risk your finances and your career when you're in your twenties and need a modest amount of money to survive (and perhaps can call on family help or return to the conventional workforce), but it's quite another when your kids are in private school, you have mortgage payments, and you want to drive imported sports cars. I've seen people take early risks and then "settle in," content and complacent on a plateau that continues to decline as technology, methodology, competition, society, and the economy move and they don't. You don't reach higher levels of professional and personal success by choosing to stop climbing.

- *Ego.* There is a continuing reward from which you cannot wean yourself. A few clients continue to use you in the same way and constantly sing your praises. You have a regular column or conference or "model" that you are lauded for. Your name is associated with a certain effort or outcome. Your ego needs are threatened if you have to abandon or replace some of these ongoing "parades" in order to reach new ground.

- *Comfort.* Some coaches walk through their work blindfolded or multitasking because they've achieved a high level of methodological success and needn't work all that hard. It's sort of like my determining that there were basically 11 conditions that I was facing 99 percent of the time in organizational development consulting, except that I found that to be boring and had to move on. But many people find that condition to be a great rocking chair, and move back and forth while going nowhere. When you get too comfortable in your work, you're coasting, not pumping.

- *Norms.* If you have vestiges of self-esteem issues, then you can be unduly influenced by others and by the norms of the profession. You tend to move with the crowd and are the antithesis of an "early adopter"— you become a herd animal. You are quick to do what others find is right for the majority, which will never, ever place you in the minority that constitutes the leading edge.

- *Anality.* This is a word I've focused on, but there is a need to be bodacious here. This is a fixation on input and task instead of outcome and result. Hence, a coach focuses on fine-tuning the questions in an assessment tool, or changing the interview sequence, or trying new technology in recording the client's behavior. People who grow and move rapidly strive for faster, more dramatic results, not better and better details on the methodology. Dramatic growth requires a telescope, not a microscope.

- *Confinement.* To reach the highest levels of any profession, but particularly helping professions such as coaching, you must be prepared to provide your value in diverse offerings to as wide an array of people as possible. That will require that you test and experiment with remote devices, audio and video, books that are hard-copy and electronic, online communities, licensing your intellectual property, and so on. You can't confine yourself to what worked well two days ago. YOU have to be in the advance guard of what will work well two days from now.

> *Stop It! If you haven't offered your value in new ways over the past year, and if you haven't developed new interactions and initiatives, then you're simply following others, which will never put you in front.*

The following recommendations are specifically intended to help you reach the highest levels of the coaching profession. Not all of you will get there, but that's a question of your talent and discipline. Those of us who are striving to reach the pinnacle realize that it's a moving target—created by all of us who are climbing.

ALAN'S TECHNIQUES TO REACH NEW LEVELS OF COACHING SUCCESS

1. *Abandon some clients.* Yes, you read that correctly. At this stage of your career, you have clients who have been with you for a long time—too long. They are no longer that profitable, you're charging them far lower fees than you would new clients, and you've kept them on as if they are lucky charms or out of a distorted loyalty.

   I say "distorted" because you're probably not helping them as much as you used to: the work is uninteresting, the settings are overly familiar, and it may even be a codependency at this point.

   Every year, or two at most, you should consider "dropping" the bottom 15 percent of your business. You can do this gracefully by pointing out what I already have: you're not serving them as well as others might, you don't want to raise the fees you are charging them, and it's appropriate at this point to disengage. Some of the indicators are

   • The business is boring.

   • Your revenues and profits are stagnant.

   • You bring no distinguishing assets that others couldn't bring.

   • There is no referral work originating with the client any more.

This may seem tough, but you can't reach out to new heights unless you let go of old baggage. And, you're doing the client a favor as well.

2. *Create new approaches, don't adopt them.* We've established the tremendous impact of intellectual capital transformed into intellectual property. And we've questioned, "Who certifies the certifier?" The result of these musings is that you're as well positioned as anyone to initiate new approaches and devices.

Part of your time should be devoted to developing new coaching methodologies that will help improve your market gravity and fees, and develop you as an object of interest and a thought leader. For example, can you create an Internet chat room where your clients can talk anonymously? Can you create an "internal coaching manual" to help clients develop their own cadre of coaches? Can you write an article on the differences between coaching and mentoring?

Being well read and well versed in the profession and knowing what's going on in terms of the state of the art is important in one's growth. But in reaching new levels of success, *setting the state of the art* is the distinguishing feature of those on the next plateau. Take the responsibility and time to create, test, publicize, and implement new methods to help clients and advance the profession.

3. *Don't be afraid to be a critic of the mainstream.* There's a difference between sniping and constructive engagement. There's a difference between sour grapes and learned opposition.

In any profession—and coaching is certainly no exception—bad practices develop, charlatans emerge, and lousy ideas are touted by the uninitiated (or the unethical and malicious). Coaching is unregulated. The fact that anyone can claim to be a coach is both a blessing (ease of entry) and a curse (schlock abounds). Clients do NOT look at coaching credentials and initials after one's name. They seek trusting relationships, which, alas, some people can establish without any content behind them.

Think of Willy Loman at best and Bernie Madoff at worst.

You don't get to high altitudes without passing others on the way up (and don't listen to the nonsense about coming down again), and you have to do that in many cases by being critical of their gear and their technique. If you're afraid to stand out in a crowd, then, by definition, you'll always be part of the pack. The most important thing about reaching the highest levels of success is that you are fearless in supporting the best and condemning the worst.

Are many evaluation tools merely horoscopes? Are some interviewing techniques wandering and worthless? Do some coaches inappropriately take the role of unlicensed therapists?

If you don't speak out, as a leader in the profession, then others will. And they will be the ones who are considered to be the leaders.

Every star performer in any discipline I've ever met is constantly striving to be better, not merely to maintain the status quo. The key element of that mentality is to understand that success trumps perfection every time.

Every time.

SUCCESS, NOT PERFECTION

There are three deadly sins in coaching. I used to believe that one was undercapitalization, but I was dead wrong. It's always amazing to reflect on how stupid I was two weeks ago.

One sin is poor self-esteem. We've covered that in some detail already.

The second sin is refusing to see this profession as a business, and treating it as an avocation—a "calling"—and not an occupation. This book is about the business of coaching.

The third I want to address here in some detail, although I've alluded to it earlier: life is about success, not about perfection. This is an invidious and critical error that creeps into too many professionals' lives.

If you combine these three sins, by the way, you have a dynamic wherein you can never succeed enough. No matter what you accomplish, you will hear from others and/or from yourself:

- That was a terrific project, but not as good as the one you did last year for Acme.
- People were really impressed, even though Jones is still the legend for his work 10 years ago.
- You helped him a great deal, although I was hoping that we would conclude a week earlier.
- She's raving about your work, although she does tend to become overly enthusiastic when she's been helped.
- You did almost as well as I might have done myself.

You get the idea. There is always a higher goal, a more distant shore, a more difficult challenge that you could have achieved or surmounted.

And that's a lot of crap.

You need to throw this baggage off the train. Don't just drop it, because it will still be on the same train traveling at the same speed. Throw it out into the countryside. If you kill a few cows, so be it.

> *Stop It! If life were about perfection, no plane would ever fly, no speech would ever be completed, no life would ever be improved. And no one would ever be happy.*

A therapist was the first to use the phrase on me. He said, after I was complaining about not going fast enough, or high enough, or far enough, "Alan, for goodness sake, life is about success, not perfection." And the vapors lifted, the air cleared, and I was healed! (Not perfectly, but successfully.)

And all that for $110 an hour! (I told him never to read my books about value-based fees.)

So, what will this afflatus do for you? Well, once you decide that success is sufficient, and that "perfect 10s" are both rare and subjective (would you trust your wallet to a gymnastics judge?), you can "settle for success." That includes the following benefits, in terms of accelerating your climb to higher levels of this profession:

1. *Far, far less labor intensity.* Most excess work is invested in the quest for perfection. These are the people who insist on cleaning remote parts of their cars with tiny cotton swabs instead of being content with washing it in a tenth of the time. The quest for perfection is what drives you past rational work levels with clients, which has a serious impact on your discretionary time and your profit margins.

2. *The ability to move much more rapidly.* You'll be able to start sooner and end faster, beating the competition and delighting your clients. Figure 10-3 shows what that looks like.

In Figure 10-3, when you're about 80 percent ready, you MOVE! After that, the highest levels of time demands occur, with diminishing returns in effectiveness. Another 20 percent spent on this book would be unnoticed by you; an additional 20 percent invested in a speech is lost on the audience; 20 percent more in a coaching assignment will impress neither the buyer nor the client qualitatively.

Moreover, in most of life's endeavors, we fine-tune as we go. I've never had a project of any kind that ran a course consistent with what was predicted at the outset. Things change, and we adjust, which is how the final 20 percent can be accommodated if it is required.

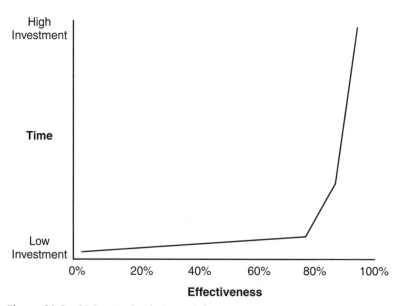

Figure 10-3   80 Percent Ready, Move Rule

(You may tell me that aircraft and space shuttles don't stop at 80 percent, but I assure you that they do, or they'd never leave the ground. That's why they have three redundant systems, not none, and not six.)

3. *Reduced stress levels.* The two greatest causes of stress—and the emotional and physical illnesses that stress causes—are

- The belief that one doesn't know what will happen tomorrow

- The belief that one has no influence over what will happen tomorrow

These stress factors are intensified when you strive for perfection, because you can bet the family farm that you will not reach perfection in most circumstances. Hence, the need to be realistic and rational, to accept that you can make very intelligent estimates of tomorrow's events, and then decide what you can influence locally in your best interests.

An Air Force colonel who was a client of mine in Hawaii explained to me once that efficiency would require 25 planes to destroy an enemy target; effectiveness would call for 50, just to make sure; but perfection would require an infinite number of aircraft. (Air Force colonels tend to talk this way.) He always opted for the effective number, since the Air Force's charter was to be effective, not efficient, but also certainly not perfect.

I found the man totally unstressed!

4. *You don't really know what perfection is, so you'll avoid pursing a chimera.* Dorothy Parker, the great Algonquin Round Table wit, said once, "If you teach a cannibal to use a fork, is that really progress?"

What is perfection? Does your client deal with the media better, or must the client deal with them as well as a press secretary would? Does your client encourage and motivate better, or must the client be as good as Knute Rockne, the legendary Notre Dame football coach, or Vince Lombardi, the Green Bay Packers coach, or Teddy Roosevelt, leading his Rough Riders up San Juan Hill? Where does it end? What is perfect?

In baseball, there is a phenomenon known as a "perfect game," wherein the pitcher allows no hits and no walks, and there have been only about 40 in history. However, a perfect game demands no base runners, so the fielders cannot make an error, either. Yet, the pitcher can make any number of pitches. Shouldn't a perfect game be only 27 pitches, one to each opposing batter (who, presumably, swing and hit the ball at a fielder)? Or perhaps 81 pitches, meaning that each batter was struck out on three pitches without touching the ball?

Of course, that's never been done in millions of games. But isn't that "perfection"? Truthfully, I don't know, and neither do you, and neither does the commissioner of baseball. Nor does he care, and I can't blame him.

What I'm trying to get across is that, counterintuitively, the search for perfection leads to anything but. It won't drive you to a higher level, and it's not the point at all. The point is to do your level best, to keep improving your skills, and to keep getting better. As you can see, in that sequence, there is no terminal. There is no end to the journey.

There is no perfection.

But there is success. And once you've achieved it, what do you do with it in the larger scheme of things? What's your legacy to be?

Even I can't tell you that. But you can make those decisions if you're not busy chasing the siren song of perfection.

CREATING LEGACIES

Once you reach the heights in any profession, the question that's always been present but now seems to take more definitive shape as you climb through the fog is: what's next?

In the book *The Navigator*, author Morris West writes, "And that's the terror of the high place, and the high man: Is it God he hears or only the echo of his own mad shouting?"[1] We have to be careful about locking ourselves into such a small, self-imposed world that all we breathe is our own exhaust.

The remedy for that is one's legacy. A legacy is typically considered to be the representation of how one is remembered and what one leaves behind. But I'd like to suggest that legacies are continua, not fixed points. You are creating legacies all the time. However, once you reach the "high place," you're able to examine, understand, and manage the process much more deliberately.

Nor is this too grand a belief or position. Creating a legacy shouldn't be for you—which would be extremely egocentric, like people who plan their own funerals and are buried in their Cadillac—but for others. It's a continuation of your helping nature, which is more in line with being a coach than with most other professions.

---

[1] My habit is to quote authors exactly, and not to change or neutralize pronouns. I respect my readers and believe you'll make proper accommodation.

In other words, who would be better than a highly successful and effective coach to create and leave lasting measures of help and support?

There are various ways to leave your mark and that help, but I'm suggesting that it's better to start now and consciously, rather than to allow your contributions to be remembered or utilized by default. Peter Drucker wrote a novel, but his huge contribution has been the virtual creation of the practice of management and certainly of strategy. He left a surfeit of works to ensure that we remember and are helped by his wisdom in our work, and not merely the enjoyment of his novel.

Figure 10-4 shows the output of another superb management thinker, the social psychologist Abraham Maslow: his pyramid.

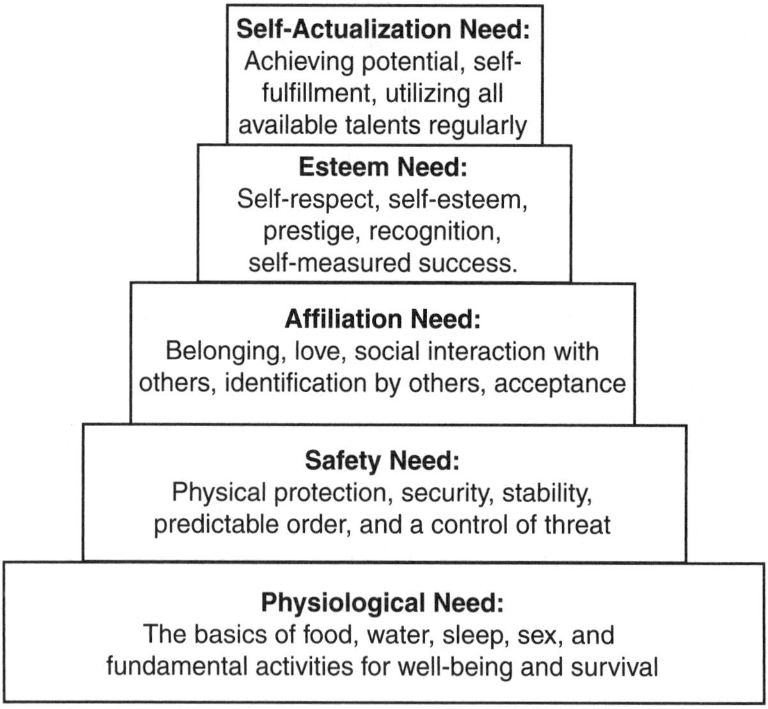

Self-Actualization Need:
Achieving potential, self-fulfillment, utilizing all available talents regularly

Esteem Need:
Self-respect, self-esteem, prestige, recognition, self-measured success.

Affiliation Need:
Belonging, love, social interaction with others, identification by others, acceptance

Safety Need:
Physical protection, security, stability, predictable order, and a control of threat

Physiological Need:
The basics of food, water, sleep, sex, and fundamental activities for well-being and survival

Figure 10-4   Maslow's Hierarchy of Needs

At this stage of your career, you're at the self-actualization level. But "self-fulfillment" and the utilization of existing talents (and continually acquired talents, one would hope) isn't so easily addressed.

That's where legacy comes into the picture. The more you consciously create and deliver intellectual property, ideas, and incentive to grow to others, the more you'll be able to fulfill yourself where external and artificial means cannot. Whether that involves monetary gain or not *is immaterial*. Legacy doesn't imply "free." It implies "lasting" and "useful" and "important."

> *Stop It! Never underestimate or downplay your impact on others. Being cognizant of your contributions and your legacy, as we define it here, actually helps you become still more effective as you deal with more and more sophisticated needs.*

With that preface, here are some examples of legacy areas for the highly successful professional coach.

Published and Spoken Record

There is, today, a Dale Carnegie "app" for the iPhone, iPad, and other platforms. Dale Carnegie was born in 1888, 23 years after the end of the Civil War, and died in 1955, before color television and satellites. Yet his words and approaches are readily available today, even on the most sophisticated technological media. And his concepts are still embraced by millions. (One can make the same case about Napoleon Hill, Earl Nightingale, and scores of others.)

What you put in writing or record on various media lasts. Or, perhaps more accurately, has the potential to last. Think about writing and speaking "for the ages." Don't necessarily link your points to contemporary events (everyone is tired of hearing about the original Tylenol crisis, and the Gulf oil rig disaster will be at least a year old by the time you read this). Strive for *process* points about coaching and helping others (e.g., don't believe that someone is damaged unless you see evidence to support such a belief), not *content* (e.g., here's how you coach in the buggy whip industry).

You're in a position to give some careful thought to the historical record you're in the midst of leaving. I'm not being grandiloquent here, and you shouldn't be intimidated by the reality of it. You're leaving your legacy every day when you write and speak, no less than I am here on these pages.

Do you want to be known and remembered for your current messages, or do you want to change them?

Involvement in the Profession

There are two separate quotes I've found that are interesting when juxtaposed:[2]

> History is only the biography of great men.
> —Thomas Carlyle

> There are no great men, only great challenges that ordinary men are forced by circumstances to meet.
> —Admiral William F. Halsey

I find these interesting because they are probably both very accurate, with few exceptions. History, therefore, com-

[2] See footnote 1.

prises the biographies of all of us, and some of us rise to take on certain challenges, often ones that others can't or won't.

Professions aren't plants or animals, with preprogrammed DNA that manages to perpetuate the species and tends to ensure growth and size consistent with the organism. Professions are fungible and fickle. Their infrastructure tends to change, often as a result of external forces. At the height of the 1990s economic boom, professional architects were one of the very few professions in the country to suffer a net decline in income each year. That's because they didn't (and still don't) charge for their value, and they allowed general contractors and designers to erode what was once their exclusive territory.

They neither blew their own horns nor stopped breathing their own exhaust.

For a profession to prosper and endure, those who are most successful can't remove themselves from the fray, and pose as monks in lofty monasteries dealing with metaphysical mysteries. We have to enter the fray down in the trenches, and rub shoulders with our colleagues who are trying to advance.

We all have to contribute to the profession, which I consider a moral duty once we are successful. (This is why discretionary time is wealth—if you don't have time to devote to the profession, you can't create your legacy. It's not about merely donating money.)

We can contribute—pay back—by

- Appearing at professional association and professional community activities
- Creating and disseminating best practices of the profession
- Serving as an exemplar and model
- Mentoring and/or coaching others

- Accepting and developing interns
- Teaching the craft at schools of higher learning
- Serving as spokespeople for the profession
- Identifying and publicly criticizing unprofessional practices
- Producing ongoing blogs and newsletters with state-of-the-art information

You get the idea. You should place yourself in the position of publicly defending, developing, and perpetuating the profession. When enough public figures participate in this manner, professions grow and evolve, and all ships rise with the tide.

I thought it fitting to conclude the book with these admittedly strong goals and aspirations. Because not only is that what we're capable of in this profession, but it is in reality our true calling.

None of us—not you, not me—is here to stick a toe in the water.

We're here to make waves.

WHAT'S MY COACH QUOTIENT (CQ)?

Y OU'RE PROBABLY A BETTER, more experienced coach than you think! There are no "correct answers" to this assessment; just answer honestly and see where your strengths are.

1. Who has asked me for help or assistance in the past?

_____

_____

_____

_____

2. Why did they choose me?

_____

_____

_____

_____

3. What were the topics or issues?

_____

_____

_____

_____

4. What did I do or advise to help them?

_____

_____

_____

_____

5. What was the result?

_____

_____

_____

_____

6. What did I learn from this?

_____

_____

_____

_____

7. How can I use these experiences in my future coaching?

_____

_____

_____

_____

101 QUESTIONS FOR ANY SALES SITUATION YOU'LL EVER FACE

AN OVERVIEW

This material is intended to provide questions that you can ask in virtually any sales situation, thereby

1. Maintaining a conversational and "nonsales" approach
2. Keeping the other party talking in order to learn
3. Avoiding "deselection" by volunteering very little yourself
4. Finding the buyer, building a relationship, and closing business
5. Accelerating the entire sales process

The next few pages provide the opportunity for you to customize the questions to fit your particular type of sale, niche, specialty, or customer. I strongly advise that you personalize the generic questions so that they support your particular practice or business.

You might choose to take this manual on calls, to keep it by the phone, or to use it as the basis for printing out your own questions to keep in your briefcase or calendar. The copyright is intended to protect the work as it is presented, and to avoid resale or unethical use. However, you should feel free to incorporate the generic questions and the derivations that flow from them into your personal routine and support materials.

The questions are deliberately overlapping, and stop just short of being duplicative. Essentially, you want to elicit the same information in as many diverse ways as possible.

A FEW GUIDELINES FOR USE

- Don't interrogate people. It's seldom necessary to ask even the majority of the questions in any one category.
- Employ follow-up questions. The questions contained herein are "triggers" that may engender a response that demands further clarification.
- Trust is essential for candor. The other party will be most honest and responsive when trust has been established (i.e., they believe that you have their best interests in mind).
- Never be content with a single question, no matter how satisfying the answer appears to be. Some people will attempt to deceive you to save their ego, and others will inadvertently deceive you because they misunderstood the question. I recommend that you use at least three questions per category if the answers are consistent, and six or more if the answers appear to be inconsistent.

These questions are rational, objective, and, most of all, based on common sense and simple discourse. Try not to be distracted or to digress until the answer you're seeking in any given category is forthcoming. For example, it's dysfunctional to ask questions about objectives if you haven't asked the questions that can satisfy you that you're talking to an economic buyer. Discipline is best.

Ironically, the more time you take to find the right answers, the more you accelerate the business.

Good selling and good luck!

—Alan Weiss, Ph.D.

I. QUALIFYING THE PROSPECT

This is the process of determining whether the inquiry is appropriate for your business in terms of size, relevance, seriousness, and related factors. In other words, you don't want to pursue a lead that can't result in legitimate—and worthwhile—business.

Questions:

1. Why do you think we might be a good match?
2. Is there budget allocated for this project?
3. How important is this need (on a scale of 1 to 10)?
4. What is your timing to accomplish this?
5. Who, if anyone, is demanding that this be accomplished?
6. How soon are you willing to begin?
7. Have you made a commitment to proceed, or are you still analyzing?
8. What are your key decision criteria in choosing a resource?

9. Have you tried this before (will this be a continuing endeavor)?

10. Is your organization seeking formal proposals for this work?

Key Point: You want to determine whether the potential work is large enough to merit your involvement, relevant to your expertise, and near enough on the horizon to merit rapid responsiveness.

II. FINDING THE ECONOMIC BUYER

The economic buyer is the person who can write a check in return for your value contribution. He or she is the ONLY buyer you should be concerned about. Contrary to a great deal of poor advice, the economic buyer is virtually *never* in human resources, training, meeting planning, or related support areas.

Questions:

11. Whose budget will support this initiative?

12. Who can immediately approve this project?

13. To whom will people look for support, approval, and credibility?

14. Who controls the resources required to make this happen?

15. Who has initiated this request?

16. Who will claim responsibility for the results?

17. Who will be seen as the main sponsor and/or champion?

18. Do you have to seek anyone else's approval?

19. Who will accept or reject proposals?
20. If you and I were to shake hands, could I begin tomorrow?

Key Point: The larger the organization, the greater the number of economic buyers. They need not be the CEO or owner, but they must be able to authorize and produce payment. Committees are *never* economic buyers.

III. REBUTTING OBJECTIONS

"Obstacles are those terrible things you see when you take your eyes off the goal," said philosopher Hannah Arendt. Objections are a sign of interest. Turn them around to your benefit. Once you demolish objections, there is no longer a reason not to proceed in a partnership.

Questions (in response to an economic buyer's objections):

21. Why do you feel that way? (Get at the true cause.)
22. If we resolve this, can we then proceed? (Is this the sole objection?)
23. But isn't that exactly why you need me? (The reversal approach.)
24. What would satisfy you? (Make the buyer answer the objection.)
25. What can we do to overcome that? (Demonstrate joint accountability.)
26. Is this unique? (Is there precedent for overcoming it?)
27. What's the consequence? (Is it really serious or merely an annoyance?)

28. Isn't that low probability? (Worry about likelihoods, not the remote.)

29. Shall I address that in the proposal? (Let's focus on value.)

30. Why does it even matter in light of the results? (The ROI is the point.)

Key Points: Don't be on the defensive and try to slay each objection with your sword, or you'll eventually fall on it. Embrace the buyer in the "solutions," and demonstrate that some objections are insignificant when compared with benefits (e.g., there will always be some unhappy employees in any change effort).

IV. ESTABLISHING OBJECTIVES

Objectives are the *outcomes* that represent the client's desired and improved conditions. They are never inputs (e.g., reports, focus groups, manuals), but rather always outputs (e.g., increased sales, reduced attrition, improved teamwork). Clear objectives prevent "scope creep" and enable a rational engagement and disengagement to take place, resulting in much greater consulting efficiency and profit margins. (Note that items IV, V, and VI—objectives, measures, and value—are the basis of conceptual agreement.)

Questions:

31. What is the ideal outcome you'd like to experience?

32. What results are you trying to accomplish?

33. What better product/service/customer condition are you seeking?

34. Why are you seeking to do this (work/project/ engagement)?

35. How would the operation be different as a result of this work?

36. What would be the return on investment (sales, assets, equity, etc.)?

37. How would your image/repute/credibility be improved?

38. What harm (e.g., stress, dysfunction, turf wars, and so on) would be alleviated?

39. How much would you gain on the competition as a result?

40. How would your value proposition be improved?

Key Points: Most buyers know what they *want* but not necessarily what they *need*. By pushing the buyer on the end results, you are helping to articulate and formalize the client's perceived benefits, thereby increasing your own value in the process. Without clear objectives, you do not have a legitimate project.

V. ESTABLISHING METRICS

Metrics are measures of progress toward the objectives that enable you and the client to ascertain the rate and totality of success. They assign proper credit to you and your efforts, and also signify when the project is complete (objectives are met) and it is proper to disengage.

Questions:

41. How will you know that we've accomplished your intent?

42. How, specifically, will the operation be different when we're done?

43. How will you measure this?

44. What indicators will you use to assess our progress?

45. Who or what will report on our results (against the objectives)?

46. Do you already have measures in place that you intend to apply?

47. What is the rate of return (on sales, investment, etc.) that you are seeking?

48. How will we know how the public, employees, and/or customers perceive it?

49. Each time we talk, what standard will tell us that we're progressing?

50. How would you know it if you tripped over it?

Key Points: Measures can be subjective, so long as you and the client agree on who is doing the measuring and how. For example, the buyer's observation that he or she is called upon less to settle "turf" disputes and has fewer complaints from direct reports aimed at colleagues are valid measures for the objective of "improved teamwork."

VI. ASSESSING VALUE

Determining the value of the project for the client's organization is *the* most critical aspect of conceptual agreement and pre-proposal interaction. That's because when the buyer stipulates to significant value, the fee is placed in proper perspective (ROI) and is seldom an issue of contention. Conversations with the buyer should *always* focus on value and *never* on fee or price.

Questions:

51. What will these results mean for your organization?

52. How would you assess the actual return (ROI, ROA, ROS, ROE, or some other metric)?

53. What would be the extent of the improvement (or correction)?

54. How will these results affect the bottom line?

55. What are the *annualized* savings (the first year might be deceptive)?

56. What is the intangible impact (e.g., on repute, safety, or comfort)?

57. How would you, personally, be better off or better supported?

58. What is the scope of the impact (on customers, employees, vendors)?

59. How important is this compared to your overall responsibilities?

60. What if this fails?

Key Points: Subjective value (stress alleviated) can be every bit as important as more tangible results (higher sales). Never settle for "Don't worry, it's important." Find out *how* important, because that will dictate the acceptable fee range.

VII. DETERMINING THE BUDGET RANGE

In the absence of a general understanding about how much the prospect intends to invest (prior to understanding the full value proposition), too much guessing takes place. In many cases, the budget is fixed and entirely inappropriate, and in others it represents a better understanding of the ROI than the one the consultant has! (Don't forget, this presupposes that you're talking to an economic buyer.)

Questions:

61. Have you arrived at a budget or investment range for this project?
62. Are funds allocated, or must they be requested?
63. What is your expectation of the investment required?
64. So we don't waste time, are there parameters to remain within?
65. Have you done this before, and at what investment level?
66. What are you able to authorize during this fiscal year?
67. Can I assume that a strong proposition will justify proper expenditure?
68. How much are you prepared to invest to gain these dramatic results?
69. For a dramatic return, will you consider a larger investment?
70. Let's be frank: what are you willing to spend?

Key Points: There is nothing wrong with exceeding the budget expectation if you muster a strong enough value proposition. But don't even proceed with a proposal if the prospect has a seriously misguided expectation of the investment need, or simply has an inadequate, fixed budget.

VIII. PREVENTING UNFORESEEN OBSTACLES

As comedienne Gilda Radner used to say, "It's always some-thing." Inevitably, it seems, the best-laid plains are undermined by objections, occurrences, and serendipity from left field. For-tunately, there are questions that can establish some preventive actions against even the unforeseen.

Questions:

71. Is there anything we haven't discussed that could get in the way?

72. In the past, what has occurred to derail potential projects like this?

73. What haven't I asked you that I should have about the environment?

74. What do you estimate the probability is of our going forward?

75. Are you surprised by anything I've said or that we've agreed upon?

76. At this point, are you still going to make this decision yourself?

77. What, if anything, do you additionally need to hear from me?

78. Is anything likely to change in the organization in the near future?

79. Are you awaiting the results of any other initiatives or decisions?

80. If I get this proposal to you tomorrow, how soon will you decide?

Key Points: Make sure that your project isn't contingent upon other events transpiring (or not transpiring). If the buyer is holding out on you, these questions will make it more difficult for him or her to dissemble. Build into your proposal benefits to outweigh the effects of any external factors.

IX. INCREASING THE SIZE OF THE SALE

Once conceptual agreement is gained, it makes sense to capitalize on the common ground and strive for the largest possible relationship. Most consultants don't obtain larger contracts *because they don't ask for or suggest them.* You can't possibly lose anything by attempting to increase the business at this juncture.

Questions:

81. Would you be amenable to my providing a variety of options?

82. Is this the only place (division, department, geography) applicable?

83. Would it be wise to extend this through implementation and oversight?

84. Should we plan to also coach key individuals who are essential to the project?

85. Would you benefit from benchmarking against other firms?

86. Would you also like an idea of what a retainer might look like?

87. Are there others in your position with like needs who I should see?

88. Do your subordinates possess the skills to support you appropriately?

89. Should we run focus groups/other samplings to test employee reactions?

90. Would you like me to test customer response at various stages?

Key Points: If you don't ask, you don't get. Don't throw everything including the kitchen sink into your proposal in an attempt to justify your fee. Instead, "unbundle" what you're capable of providing and add the various items back in for an additional fee.

X. GOING FOR THE CLOSE

You're on the home stretch, but not across the finish line. Runners who slow down as they approach the tape lose to someone else with a better late "kick." Run through the tape at full speed by driving the conversation right through the close of the sale and the check clearing the bank.

Questions:

91. If the proposal reflects our last discussions, how soon can we begin?

92. Is it better to start immediately, or wait for the first of the month?

93. Is there anything at all preventing our working together at this point?

94. How rapidly are you prepared to begin once you see the proposal?

95. If you get the proposal tomorrow, can I call Friday at 10 for approval?

96. While I'm here, should I begin some of the preliminary work today?

97. Would you like to shake hands and get started, with proposal to follow?

98. Do you prefer a corporate check or to wire the funds electronically?

99. May I allocate two days early next week to start my interviews?

100. Can we proceed?

Key Points: There is never a better time than when you're in front of the buyer and he or she is in agreement and excited about the project. Even without a proposal, beginning immediately "pours cement" on the conceptual agreement and greatly diminishes the possibility of your being derailed by surprise.

XI. THE MOST VITAL QUESTION

All of the preceding 100 questions are actually based on the reaction to one question that we often fail to ask of the most difficult person of all. And unlike most of the prior inquiries, it's a simple binary question, with a clear yes or no response.

Question:

101. Do you believe it yourself?

Key Point: The first sale is always to yourself.

INTERVIEWS
WITH COACHES

I'VE ASKED A SMALL GROUP of excellent coaches to share their views on various challenges and requirements of the profession. I think you'll find their suggestions, experiences, and insights to be of great value. Great professionals give back to the profession, and I'm honored that these coaches have made these contributions for our benefit.

INTERVIEW 1

Suzanne Bates
President and CEO, Bates Communications
Wellesley, Massachusetts

What is the most difficult aspect of coaching executives and senior people?

The most difficult aspect of coaching senior people is sustaining commitment. The beginning of a coaching relationship is a lot like dating—initially, clients fall in love with you, or at least with the idea of having a coach. They can't wait to see you, set aside time, and want to talk about everything. They are delighted to have a partner on their journey—someone who actually cares about their career.

As time goes on, some clients become like bad lovers. They stop calling; they cancel dates or show up distracted by their other paramour—the job or the company. They realize that coaching takes commitment. They may complain about having to choose between their job and their coaching. Make sure that your coaching meetings are aligned with the demands on them. You have to focus on their business priorities. It is useless to scold or cajole them, or to remind them why they hired you. You can't force the chef to learn a new recipe when his kitchen is on fire.

Stay on top of the client's calendar. Prior to every meeting, check in. Find out what is taking up space in his head. See what's ahead in the next few weeks. Even if you'd planned to work on a board presentation, if she has an employee crisis or a breakdown in the supply chain, address that first. Get agreement up front about how to spend your time together. Crisis is an opportunity, not an interruption. Put yourself squarely into the client's world, and connect business priorities to professional development. Tune in and be ruthlessly relevant.

Clients make the initial commitment to coaching when it is in their self-interest to do so. They remain committed over time when it remains in their self-interest. Of course, as a coach, you need to develop a trusting relationship, be regarded as their intellectual equal, and be creative in utilizing all the skills and tools you have. You can also get and keep commitment with quick wins and periodic reviews of progress. Great feedback from the boss on a presentation; getting the team to work together—these are milestones that you need to talk about and evaluate regularly.

Occasionally, the commitment is never really made. If there's too much time between agreement and the first coaching session, or if the client is stressed or business issues are changing rapidly, the client may question her initial commitment to coaching. Get started right away, and stay focused on what's happening right now. Make it easy to commit initially, and then build on small successes. It's never a good idea to enter into a coaching relationship with a reluctant client, but if you find yourself in that situation, tools like the 360-degree feedback interviews and report can be a catalyst; there's nothing like hearing how others see you to get you motivated. Ultimately, if you can overcome these hurdles and sustain commitment over a period of months, you'll build a reputation as a coach who gets results.

What is the best way to disengage and end a coaching relationship?
The secret to ending a coaching relationship is to plan how it will end from the beginning. You should never start a coaching assignment thinking that it will never end, even though a great coaching assignment can lead to a lifelong relationship. At the beginning you must define goals and timelines to create urgency and momentum. Otherwise the coaching drags on, morphs into new, unanticipated assignments, and loses focus.

There are three dangers in starting a coaching engagement without the end goals and an end date in mind. First, there is no urgency. That puts the onus on the coach to create momentum and work miracles. The second danger is rapid disengagement. Clients won't stay in it if they can't see the finish line. This often results in a bad "breakup." And it hurts about as badly as losing your high school sweetheart. The third danger is that your reputation will suffer. If you don't know where you're going, you don't get results, and ultimately you fail to get the references you need if you are to grow and sustain a successful coaching practice.

Ending well requires investing up front. Many clients want to jump in because they have urgent needs. It's fine to get started, but simultaneously you need to win agreement on goals, timelines, outcomes, and measurements of success. This will be your road map, and it will keep your client and you on track when new challenges threaten to derail the engagement. You can always renew the engagement after six months or a year. If the coaching program was a success, you get the client to articulate the value, reset goals, and pick up where you left off. This is paramount for the client's satisfaction and your professional reputation.

If a client wants to end it before it's over, this is usually because he isn't seeing results or the results aren't closely aligned with what's important to him. We strongly recommend that our clients have a trusted advisor, boss, or mentor engaged in the process to provide them with accurate feedback and remind them of their goals periodically. If they consult with an advisor, they'll often recommit. If you are coaching the CEO, it may be difficult to get him or her to engage a trusted advisor. Many top executives are isolated. However, the more they can engage others to support their coaching programs, the more likely they are to stay engaged and reach the finish line. Others besides you can help them see how far they've come.

To avoid abrupt endings, our firm offers a "coaching assurance" program, which provides more limited access to the coach for an additional six months or one year. You can set new goals or complete work on the goals you already had. And, even when the coaching engagement ends, the relationship should not. We schedule an ROI interview with a client and/or the client company six months after we wrap up. Get your clients on the phone and interview them about the value they derived;

they are very likely to engage you again for another project or refer friends and colleagues.

What if you want to end the relationship? There are plenty of reasons to do it, though these situations should be rare if you follow your process. You should fire your client if he or she behaves unethically, refuses to pay, or refuses to meet other contractual obligations, such as missing more than one or two meetings without cause. It is a waste of your time and not likely to change. A client is also within his or her right to end a coaching program if the coach behaves unethically, works at cross-purposes, discusses privileged information inappropriately, undermines the client's standing with the company, or does not deliver on contractual obligations.

Whenever a coaching relationship ends, it is important to celebrate. Always acknowledge the work, point out the progress, express appreciation for the client's commitment, and encourage the client to keep going. Starting well and ending well are equally essential to building your practice and feeling the satisfaction of a job well done.

INTERVIEW 2

Edward Poll, J.D., M.B.A., CMC
LawBiz® Management
Venice, California

Why are some people "uncoachable?"
Some people are busy fighting the alligators and snakes that plague them on a daily basis.

While they need an ally, a coach, to help them set their priorities, they often are so deeply involved that they can't see the forest for the trees. Even when they talk with a coach, agree on their priorities, and set dates for completion, their very next day seems to explode on them, causing them to revert to past behavior patterns.

Such people can still eventually be helped by a coach. Far tougher, however, is when you have the "know-it-all" individual. I've coached a number of lawyers who, in fact, do know a great deal. But they miss the real benefit of coaching in those situations because they are so fixed on their own ideas and perceptions. The real benefit for the lawyer is connecting with an ally, deciding together what should be done next for career advancement, and then being held accountable for the completion of the next step(s). Rather than follow this process, the "know-it-all" person typically walks away from the script that he or she has participated in developing . . . because the person "knows it all" and makes snap decisions on his or her own, disregarding the coaching process that the person enlisted in the first place.

A third challenge can come from any coaching client, and revolves around the natural human tendency to doubt the wisdom of doing something that the person has not tried before. Such people are not uncoachable, but they raise the same issues time and again. The astute coach can advance the relationship by having the answers ready.

- Client: If I seek coaching, it means I'm personally inadequate. Coach: Actually, engaging a coach means you've decided to succeed, because you'll improve more quickly than you would alone.
- Client: Engaging a coach is too expensive. Coach: Actually, coaching is an investment—in yourself. The ROI is how much more you can earn, or reduce your stress level.
- Client: I can't commit to the time that a coach demands. Coach: Actually, no commitment, no

success. The price is the time required to do what's necessary to improve.

- Client: I'm intimidated by a coach. Coach: Actually, a good coach is neither a buddy nor a bully. A coach offers leadership that compels and inspires you to be better.

- Client: Don't tell me what to do. Coach: Then why did you engage me? Get over it! Let's start to walk the same path toward your goals; you will get there faster with a coach.

What is the role or advantage of using technology in coaching?

Technology can be as basic as "smart phones" and as sophisticated as Internet meeting connections. Smart phones, for example, allow the person being coached to reach out to the coach at times that were not previously scheduled. They also allow the coach to reach out to the client from locations other than his or her office. This freedom of location and of contact serves both very well. In the case of the client, if he or she cannot reach the coach, a knee-jerk response is to question the value of the coach. Being difficult to reach does not serve the client. A stated time window within which to respond to the client needs to be developed and, more important, honored. When that occurs, even if the coach is not immediately available, the client knows that the answers to the client's challenges will be forthcoming shortly, not tomorrow or next week. Obviously, there are modifications, but that should be discussed with the client in advance, such as for vacations and other absences by the coach. And even in these circumstances, technology makes it possible to shorten or eliminate communication gaps.

Where visual aids are helpful to address the challenges that are being faced, the Internet offers us powerful tools that were not available before the current generation of technology and its visualization capabilities. Some people are visual learners, and a computer-generated diagram, graph, or flowchart can be an important tool for successful coaching.

Another example is the use of technology as a solution. An attorney told me that he was stressed because he had so much business that he was worried about inadvertently failing to do something essential for a client. We discussed his procedures for dealing with open files, and I recommended that he use a project management system that would keep track of the details. In just a week the attorney reported that the system worked so well that he had had his best night's sleep in months.

A final caveat. Technology has conspired with traditional attitudes to make many lawyers believe that they truly can go it alone. The flexibility offered by word processing and billing software, voice mail, e-mail, and other electronic tools is real, but it can become dangerous when combined with the entrepreneur's "I can manage 100 cases by myself" mentality. If the technology-fixated lawyer says of every task, "This should take me only 10 minutes to do," the result could be an overwhelmed practice that is headed either into the hands of the state bar disciplinary system or into insolvency. In this as in all other situations, the coach can be an objective sounding board.

What was your greatest coaching success and why?
There are two instances that come to mind. One is evaluated in terms of dollars, and the other is evaluated in terms of personal outcome.

First, the dollars. I was coaching a lawyer who wanted to increase her book of business in order to be on a more equal footing with her more senior partner. Although she was the law firm "managing partner," her power vis-à-vis the senior partner lacked muscle. As we discussed and planned for the usual business development tactics, the senior partner suddenly announced that he was going to retire and wanted to enter into sale/purchase negotiations with my client. We discussed the major points to be included in the agreement that she would propose, and we role-played the negotiation process. Because we were separated physically by many miles, this was a telephonic process, but it worked because of the trust and candor we had developed in our relationship. My client was well prepared and achieved her goals in the negotiation. But a problem arose: without discussing it with me, my client accepted a provision that the senior partner insisted on. When she told me about this, I replied that the agreement was great, but this provision could make it falter. Sure enough, the senior partner used it to break the agreement. My client called me in a panic on a Sunday morning, and in a 45-minute call I suggested tactics that gave her peace of mind and a road map to proceed successfully. This was an ongoing, very successful coaching relationship that was based on her trust in my advice and counsel because of my experience in the industry, and my willingness to listen to her goals and objectives and work within her comfort zone, not my own dictates.

Another successful coaching relationship helped an associate become a partner in a firm. The issues here related primarily to the relationship between my client and a supervising attorney who "pushed the hot buttons" of my client. We worked through a number of ideas and suggestions on how to respond to the challenges and unrealistic demands of the supervising attorney. After a while, I realized that we were dealing with a pattern on the part of both my client and the supervising lawyer. With the client's permission, I inquired about certain aspects of his earlier years. I was able to demonstrate that the supervising lawyer was merely the catalyst for triggering ways in which the client's own history contributed to the conflict. If my client were able to see the supervising lawyer as the catalyst to his past issues, step back a moment, and consider new ways to respond, perhaps he could change the dynamic of the relationship. Because I could see these issues with a fresh perspective and suggest options for my client to deal with them, he was able to pause, select more appropriate responses . . . and change the dynamic of the relationship. Within months thereafter, he was invited into the partnership.

INTERVIEW 3

Dr. Guido Quelle
Managing Partner, Mandat Consulting Group
Dortmund, Germany

What is the most difficult aspect of coaching executives and senior people?
Basically, there are three aspects that need to be considered to ensure successful coaching of executives or senior managers:

1. *Time available.* The time that needs to be set aside for coaching is the major hurdle that managers have to overcome once they have reached a certain level in the corporate hierarchy. The coach has to be excellent enough to justify not only the financial investment, but also the investment in time. It is important to strike a balance between formal meetings and spontaneous availability on the part of the coach, so that a client can approach the coach on the spur of the moment. Time is a question of priorities. If an executive or a senior manager recognizes that coaching helps him or her to achieve greater success in defined areas, the issue of time is no longer relevant.

2. *The coachees' experience and their success history.* Most executives and senior managers will have reached their position on the basis of past successes. This has benefits and drawbacks, since managers who have reached a certain level in the corporate hierarchy tend to assume that there is nothing left that they can (or should) learn. The number of persons who speak their minds with top-level managers openly and without ulterior motives rapidly sinks in proportion to the hierarchy level.

In addition, it is often assumed that the patterns and procedures that underlie the manager's current success will continue to lead to success in the future—which is something that cannot be taken for granted. It is imperative to question the assumption that previous experience will continue to solve future problems. A good executive coach is able to recognize previous successes, while at the same time broadening the horizon of senior-level clients by asking provocative questions.

3. *The complexity of subjects and the complexity of implementation.* The higher the client's position in the corporate hierarchy, the more complex are the subjects that are discussed with the coach. Successful executive coaching is marked by a consistent, top-down process. With the help of the coach, the client will bring order to the issues at hand and will set priorities, all the while considering the time and effort required to deal with such issues. Executives do not always want to delve in depth into all the aspects of a given topic. However, such in-depth study may become necessary from time to time—just to zoom out again and thus be able to grasp a topic in its entirety. Especially when coaching top-level executives, it is imperative to shed light also on the intrinsic effects that certain topics may have on the coach/client level.

What are the critical assets and strengths of an outstanding coach?

In the course of more than 300 different organizational development projects carried out at more than 100 national and multinational enterprises, I have been able to identify seven skills that an outstanding coach must have:

1. *Experience as a management consultant.* What good is a coach without experience as a management consultant when it comes to the successful conception and implementation of complex organization development projects? How is a coach who offers "nothing but" coaching to know the ins and outs of a company? How is he to know the topics that are mostly on the minds of his clients? Coaching is not a discipline in its own right but another aspect of consulting. A good coach offers coaching, consulting, and implementation—as and when it becomes necessary. That's when he is worth his fee.

2. *Consistent focus on the outcome.* Too many coaches focus entirely on the coaching process as such. They charge hourly rates (that are much too low) and are not really involved in their clients' targets. Fees are charged for services rendered regardless of their quality. Successful coaches concentrate exclusively on their client's targets and the outcome to be achieved. They charge a value-based fee for services provided within a given period of time—regardless of the number of meetings, phone calls, Skype calls, faxes,

e-mails, and so on exchanged over the course of a defined period. It is the result that counts.

3. *Not being a sycophant.* Top-level clients, more than other people, are surrounded by so many flatterers that they can do without more of them. An outstanding coach is courageous (and knowledgeable) enough to take and to justify an opposite standpoint. She is being uncomfortable and has to be that way. Coach and client come together not to "schmooze," but to find the path to new heights. This cannot be achieved while working with a coach who keeps nodding her head in agreement.

4. *Thinking on your feet.* An excellent coach can think extremely fast, for one thing, and for another is always able to produce an alternative that has not been taken into consideration before. This mental flexibility causes the client to start thinking in dimensions that previously appeared foreign or were not known to the client. As a result of this, valuable creativity potential is freed up.

5. *Having a sense of humor.* Humor is a proven method of dealing with a difficult situation. An excellent coach is able to laugh with the client even when—or particularly when—certain situations appear problematic at first sight. Intelligent humor has saved many a tricky moment.

6. *Being available.* Really, this is a no-brainer, but many coaches seem not to understand that the issues that coaching clients at a higher hierarchy level have to deal with cannot always be planned. There are quite a few situations where a piece of advice may be necessary or at least useful within a few hours. An

excellent coach will offer his clients various options for contacting him, and will make sure that he gets back to his clients fast—if necessary, over the weekend, while on holiday, or from overseas. Respectable clients will never abuse an offer like this.

7. *Being passionate about one's work.* A client can tell straightaway whether a coach is passionate about her work or not. However, the coach's passion is not limited to the assignment on hand; rather, it is the topic as such that the coach is just as enthusiastic about. An excellent coach is passionate about the client's success. Unfortunately, many coaches still regard their assignments as mere administrative tasks to be dealt with. That's the difference between a coach and an outstanding coach.

What are the keys in coaching entrepreneurs and business owners?

Many things that have to be considered when coaching top-level managers also come into play when coaching company owners. The problem here is that even in medium-sized and large owner-operated companies, there often is a concentration on certain individuals. Often, owner-operated companies have a structure similar to our planetary system: in the center, there is the sun, and all the planets revolve around the sun.

I know numerous companies with a turnover of several hundred million euros whose owners are treated like gods by their employees. "To be as capable in the future as the boss is today at nearly 70, that would be great," or, "It is incredible what the boss knows and can do"—these are quotations from employees that I keep hearing in owner-operated companies. The reverse conclusion is: the boss is so good that nobody even starts to try to achieve his level of performance. A dangerous fallacy.

If coaching entrepreneurs and owners is to be successful, it is important to bear in mind that the emotional link between the client and the client's own business will be much more pronounced. You can discharge a manager, but not an entrepreneur. That makes a big difference. As a rule, what an entrepreneur has on his mind is not the next step on the career ladder but his company.

It is also crucial to remember that the coach, when coaching an entrepreneur, must be familiar with committee work and must be equally able to cope with issues of corporate policy. More often than not, the coach will have to act as an intermediary between individual family members or clarify positions with the (family) advisory committee. Older entrepreneurs especially like to employ a coach specifically in order to deal with the issue of succession in the company—something that cannot be started too early, by the way. If, contrary to the assumption of the entrepreneur, the best solution is not to be found within the family, this can be a delicate issue.

An excellent entrepreneur's coach has not only the essential professional and personnel skills but also the instinct that helps her to deal with sensitive questions and knows that it takes even longer to build up trust with an entrepreneur than with a manager.

INTERVIEW 4

Kelli Richards
Tech & Music/Entertainment Consultant and Coach,
    The All Access Group
Saratoga, California

What is the role or advantage of using technology in coaching?

Technology is a wonderful thing when it comes to coaching clients. It liberates the coach, freeing him or her up to build a practice around a chosen lifestyle instead of the other way around. It enables the coach to work by phone (and the Internet) to live and work from whatever location he or she chooses. It also benefits the client in terms of faster response times (presumably) with quick feedback via e-mail between sessions, and it's a great convenience to be coached by phone rather than having to drive to meet someone.

What are the critical assets and strengths of an outstanding coach?

There are several essential attributes that are critical to being an outstanding coach. The first is emotional intelligence—being grounded as an individual, resilient, and able to assess circumstances with maturity and objectivity. I'd say that being attentive ranks highly as well. By that I mean making eye contact and using body posture (if meeting in person), listening intently to your client (free of distractions), and generally demonstrating that you're fully present, completely focused on your client and his or her issues so that it's very clear to the client that you're genuinely and sincerely committed to holding him or her accountable for achieving the desired results.

I'd also add that oftentimes you hold a vision for where the client is headed that represents greater possibilities or options than what the client can see for him- or herself.

What is the best way to disengage and end a coaching relationship?

If you don't have a fixed time period for the coaching structure, then both of you need to determine when you are complete for the time being. Among the healthier options, either the client tells you that he thinks he's done and ready to move on, OR you sense that the client has what he needs and is complete, and encourage him to move on. A healthy coaching relationship celebrates the client's wholeness and the achievement of his goals, and does not foster an unnatural dependency on the coach, but instead acknowledges and praises the client's success and personal (or professional) growth.

Both of your lives are (hopefully) enriched by the interaction and you move forward.

INTERVIEW 5

Pat Lynch, Ph.D.
President, Business Alignment Strategies, Inc.
Long Beach, California

What is your opinion of coaching "universities" and certifications?
In my opinion, most coaching "universities" and certifications are designed primarily to be moneymaking machines for those who control them. There is no widely recognized and accepted certification-granting authority in the field of coaching; rather, a myriad of people offer what they call coaching "certification" programs. In fact, many of these programs simply train people in various aspects of coaching. There is no independent organization that has identified a widely accepted and recognized body of coaching knowledge and can verify individuals' mastery of such knowledge as a prerequisite to conferring a coaching certification designation, such as is the case with the CPA designation in accounting, the CFA in financial investment, and the SPHR and PHR in human resources. Having worked closely for eight years with the Human Resources Certification Institute, an organization that has developed a widely recognized and accepted certification program for human resource professionals, I have observed firsthand the rigor that goes into creating a credible, valid certification process. The independence of the

certifying organization from the entities that offer the coaching training is a critical factor in establishing credibility. Thus, certification programs that are wedded to specific coaching training programs raise a red flag. Further, I have not seen any evidence that these coaching designations truly distinguish between those who are good coaches and those who are not.

People need to distinguish correctly between the terms *certification* and *certificate*, as they have entirely different meanings. A certificate is a piece of paper that represents the participant's attendance at a minimum number of class sessions; it indicates nothing about the individual's coaching expertise. A certification, on the other hand, is more like a diploma given to college graduates in that it must be earned by meeting accepted standards. Its designation attests that the holders have acquired a common body of knowledge in the field, have demonstrated that knowledge in a concrete, rigorous way (usually by passing a written test), and have maintained and increased their knowledge by meeting regular recertification requirements. Further, a certification indicates ongoing learning and mastery of the subject matter, and those who earn the certification often must subscribe to a code of ethics for their profession. I do not see such a widely accepted code of ethics in any of the coaching certification programs.

Until there is a widely recognized and accepted body of coaching knowledge, an independent testing organization, and a required code of ethics for coaches, no program can claim to offer a definitive coaching certification. Difficulties in establishing such acceptable standards include the lack of a coaching "function" in organizations and the sheer diversity of coaching specialties (e.g., executive coaches, life coaches, writing coaches, sports coaches). While I support the desire of individuals to learn how to be effective coaches, I would encourage them to take a close look at what a coaching "certification" designation really means, and whether it adds to their ability to be an excellent coach.

What is the best way to disengage and end a coaching relationship?

The best way to disengage and end a coaching relationship is to structure the engagement initially as a process that includes measurable outcomes along with a specific beginning and a definite end. I generally design my coaching engagements in six-month increments, which allows the time necessary for the desired changes. I do not believe in open-ended coaching assignments, which may inadvertently evolve into a codependent relationship. My goal in a coaching engagement is to have the client be measurably better off for having worked with me, not to have him or her become reliant on me for ongoing support.

Setting the expectation initially that there will be an end to the engagement reinforces the notion that our coaching arrangement is not an open-ended assignment. I establish specific objectives with clients that have measurable outcomes so that we can assess both progress and completion. Periodically reviewing these measures emphasizes the fact that there is a definite end to the relationship. I like to bring closure to the coaching engagement by taking a look back at where the client was at the beginning compared to where he or she is now, and celebrating what we have accomplished.

While I do set specific time frames for my coaching assignments, I also believe in renewing engagements when there is an explicit need to do so, and when we make a conscious decision that the extension is in the client's best interest. There generally are two scenarios. One is that the client has not achieved the desired objectives. This could be because the time frame for achieving them was (in retrospect) unrealistic, or the behaviors changed more slowly than anticipated, or things beyond the client's control legitimately took priority over the objectives. When this is the case, we make a conscious decision to renew the engagement. We then review the objectives and measures, revise them as necessary, and set another ending date. The second scenario occurs when the client has achieved the objectives and has identified additional goals that he or she would like to accomplish. When this happens, we identify new objectives and measures, and we set a specific ending date.

The disengagements of my most successful coaching assignments have been bittersweet: the clients have achieved, or made significant progress toward reaching, their goals, so our work together is done. There is a sense of pride and accomplishment about their success, yet we will miss the partnership. This situation is similar to the one I experienced at commencement time when I was a university professor: I took great pride in my students' achievements and was sorry to see (many of) them leave. Yet I knew that our work together was over, and that it was time for them to move on, better equipped to handle life's challenges and opportunities than they had been before we started. Similarly, when executives and business owners have received the help they need to improve their own conditions, it's time for them to celebrate their success and move on.

INTERVIEW 6

Linda Popky
President, Leverage 2 Market Associates
Redwood City, California

What is the role or advantage of using technology in coaching?
Technology has the potential to transform the coaching in many different ways.

In the past, we were often limited by the fact that to build a solid, trusting relationship, coaching had to be handled in person in a one-to-one manner. It took meeting together to get to know each other, to read body language and nuances, and to understand communication styles.

Travel is no longer a gating factor. Today's technological advances allow us to build that trusted relationship and capture many of those subtleties and nuances without jumping on a plane or speeding down the freeway to physically be in the same location.

Not only can we save time and money with remote coaching tools, but we can use these tools to develop as strong a bond with coaching clients long distance as we might have done through traditional methods in the past. This opens up a whole new realm of possibility in terms of global reach for coaching. We can also respond faster and more appropriately to our coaching clients, using such tools as e-mail, texting, social media, audio, and video/Webcams. Telepresence is rapidly increasing in availability and decreasing in cost, offering a very high-quality video experience for both parties.

Furthermore, technology allows the coach to watch inconspicuously from the sidelines as the individual being coached conducts himself throughout normal business interactions. We can watch, observe, and subtly suggest changes or interventions without disturbing the flow of interactions. Potential courses of action or corrective behavior can be modeled through short audios or videos, and the individual involved can be taped for future feedback.

People have very different learning styles. Some individuals are more comfortable working long distance—either over the phone or through e-mail—than they would be face to face with the coach. Others would prefer feedback delivered at arm's length through audio or video, rather than directly from a coach seated across from them.

With widely available, affordable broadband services, the cost and bandwidth of audio and video tools are no longer issues. We can now easily record interactions and conversations and play them back locally or over the Web. Inexpensive video tools like the Flip camera have taken video out of the hands of expensive third-party videographers, allowing the coach to capture the interaction quickly and effectively herself.

Furthermore, because of the rapid adoption of Web-based tools over the last several years, there is less hesitancy about or avoidance of this new technology "stuff."

Caveat emptor: do not use technology for technology's sake. We need to be careful not to jump into the adoption of technology simply because it's there, but to carefully and thoughtfully incorporate appropriate technology only when it adds value. It's critical to be careful that the coaching itself remains the key objective, and that technical advances don't overwhelm the need to improve the client's condition.

What are the keys in coaching entrepreneurs and business owners?

Entrepreneurs and owners of small businesses are a different breed of animal from managers of midsize and large organizations. To coach these individuals effectively, it's important to understand why they tend to gravitate to a start-up or small business environment.

The dynamic at the heart of a small, growing business is very different from that at a larger, more established organization. The ability to deliver a working product and close initial customer sales may weigh heavily on the mind of the entrepreneur—while he or she is simultaneously trying desperately to close the next round of financing.

The owner of a small business is usually involved intimately in many facets of the business—either because he or she likes being hands-on, or because there's no one else to delegate to. Managers at larger organizations may be more hands-off; at small companies or start-ups, they're more likely hands-on—and often up to their eyeballs in alligators.

Entrepreneurs by nature are both personal and passionate. They believe wholly and completely in their company's product and vision, and they see the company's success as a personal mission. This is *their* company, for better or for worse.

Unfortunately, many of the strengths that make these individuals such great entrepreneurs can get in the way of the business relationships and activities that are required to make the business successful in the long run. They're not comfortable with the tasks and activities required to run an ongoing business or to manage a business for explosive growth. They see themselves as leaders and visionaries, not managers.

A key inflection point comes when the organization takes outside money or venture capital. With the investment come both advice and involvement, some of which may be seen as helpful, some not. The bottom line is that there are now investors to answer to, a business to run, and exit strategies to consider.

Not all entrepreneurs are coachable. It's not that they have overwhelming faults, but that the individual isn't open to input and feedback, or ready to cede control of day-to-day issues in order to focus on bigger, more strategic activities. The most important thing a coach can do in this situation is to quickly determine whether or not he or she can improve the client's condition. If not, the company and the executive may soon part ways.

If the business owner or entrepreneur is ready and willing to accept coaching feedback, then the coach can focus on helping this person understand his or her strengths and weaknesses, become aware of where he or she is most comfortable, and identify where he or she will be asked to stretch and grow.

Ironically, the most challenging part of working with entrepreneurs may be helping them understand the ramifications of success. They need to accept the possibility that if they're wildly successful, growing their business properly may mean that they will no longer be the best person to run it. Your role as a coach is to help the individual understand the implications of growth as well as failure and be prepared to act accordingly.

How does a coach get coached?

Improvement is a lifelong effort—for coaches as well as for clients. That's why it's extremely important for coaches to continue to receive the guidance they need to improve their own behavior. In fact, I'd be wary of any coach who says that he or she no longer needs to learn or to improve his or her own performance.

I have a passion for playing classical piano music, where I find that there's so much music, yet so little time (especially when you only play in your spare time!). I know that to continue to improve, not only do I need to receive coaching and direction from teachers who are more experienced than I am, but that there is much greater value in studying with teachers who themselves study with "master teachers," teachers who regularly instruct other teachers.

That's because the direction these people receive from the master teacher not only helps them to improve their own performance, but also helps them understand how to effectively impart what they've learned to others. This, in turn, makes them more effective teachers themselves, as they continue to experience both sides of the relationship.

In the realm of the business coach, our world is changing so rapidly, with new technologies, a volatile business climate, and an ever-increasing excess of information available at our fingertips. It's virtually impossible to provide effective coaching based on only our preexisting training and knowledge—no matter how good our prior experience.

Self-knowledge is a key part of professional development, but there comes a time when all of us need the viewpoint of someone who can provide outside perspective and a different angle on a situation. Good coaches know that just as their clients benefit from coaching, so can they—for all the same reasons. The "coach's coach" has a perspective that the coach him- or herself just can't possibly have.

To be successful, coaches must find more senior, seasoned professionals whom they can trust to provide the right level of insight. The coach's coach should focus on process improvement as much as imparting content, providing direction at the right level that will enable coaches to extend their own growth and learning, while continuing to improve their clients' conditions.

INTERVIEW 7

Wayne McKinnon
The McKinnon Group
Ottawa, Canada

What is the most difficult aspect of coaching executives and senior people?
Ironically, or perhaps as expected, the people who can benefit the most from coaching are also the ones who make the least time for it or treat it as a quick hit that will have lasting results without taking the time to deal with their thoughts. These people tend to be more difficult to coach.

They move from meeting to meeting without leaving time in their schedule to contemplate what is going on around them, their role in the organization, and the input they have received.

This should not be confused with the type of person who has a quick mind, is extremely decisive, makes consistently good decisions, and yet still values input from others. This second type of person consumes very little of the coach's time but seems to derive the greatest benefit.

People of the first type need to separate the activities that require their actions, or simply their presence, from those activities where their judgment and influence are really needed and are highly valuable. Almost anyone in the organization should be capable of wordsmithing, grammar checking, and ensuring that meetings run and finish on time. Ensuring that the right things are being discussed, written about, implemented, delivered, or reported on requires someone with the greater perspective and clear judgment of the senior person.

Being honest with themselves as well as with the coach about why they are not making progress can also be a challenge that is often masked by the "I have been too busy" response. If change is required and someone wants to avoid that change, keeping busy in meetings and tasks that could easily be delegated to staff seems to be a common diversionary tactic.

Sometimes the way a person is measured contributes to this behavior. The person he or she reports to delegates to him or her tasks that the person, in turn, should delegate, but the language used or the measures in place may appear to say, "This task must be done by you." In my experience, this type of misinterpretation represents a small but important subset of people. They tend to take requests and commands too literally and fail to translate them into the true intent, which goes more like, "Here is a task that I am trusting you to have your team take care of."

Often the person simply does not have the personal or team capacity to do everything that he or she is currently trying to do, because the person either has not been decisive and strategic enough to develop the team; has not had the fortitude to focus on the best things to do versus all the things that he or she can try to do; or has not had the willingness to push back when he or she is clear on what can and cannot be done and something has to give. This is the paradox of coaching executives who can benefit the most from coaching, yet tend to be difficult to coach.

What is the funniest or oddest coaching experience you've had?

I had been working with a senior executive to help him resolve conflicts between two functional groups under his command. My client followed my guidance toward the end result of the two groups working together collaboratively to design, release, and support new services, and away from the current dysfunctional situation that had caused my client's counterpart (the leader of one of the groups) to be fired, and my client (the leader of the second group) to be promoted to his current senior executive position.

Things were progressing nicely as new processes were developed, cross-boundary relationships were nurtured, and a series of important pieces began to fall into place.

During my direct interaction with my client, we worked on ways to continue moving forward, identify measurable results that he could point to as indicators that his new approach was working, and techniques to prevent him and his organization from backsliding once I was gone.

We had worked together successfully for six months, and I really thought we had made a huge amount of progress together until the day that I reported back from the field what I had observed. In addition to the work that we had done together to make changes at his level, I noted that one of the groups that was blaming the other for delays was actually causing the delays itself, and that this could be easily fixed with a few adjustments. Moments later, I found myself unceremoniously deposited in the building lobby!

I found out later the history of the two groups under his command. My client had headed up the group that I had identified as being the cause of delays, and he had led the charge to have the leader of the other group fired and himself promoted to his senior position.

Although it was temporarily on hold, unbeknownst to me, his coup was still underway, and he was systematically planning to pick off the remaining members of the second group and replace them with members of the group that he had once led. He had come to the conclusion a long time ago that this second group contained damaged people that were causing delays and needed to be disposed of (even though together we had witnessed improvements without removing staff).

I had just unwittingly exposed to him the true cause and easy solution that would have negated the need for his misguided plan, which was certain to fail now that he knew that what he had was a process problem, not one of people. Apparently I needed to disappear quickly before anyone else found out.

INTERVIEW 8

Robbie Kellman Baxter
Peninsula Strategies
Menlo Park, California

What is the most difficult aspect of coaching executives and senior people?
I have found it easier to coach executives and other successful people for four reasons:

1. *Discipline.* They are used to working hard toward goals, and to achieving them.

2. *Responsiveness.* They understand what needs to be done and are quick to make adjustments.

3. *Flexibility.* Because they are already in a relatively senior role, they have flexibility in how they spend their time, which gives us greater freedom to make changes.

4. *Impact.* When a leader makes changes, the results can be immediate and far-flung, so the results are quickly evident, which can motivate further change.

However, working with senior people can also have unique challenges. The stakes are much higher with a senior leader, so in some cases, while the executive is quick to respond and understand the issues, he or she is unwilling to modify a behavior that has worked in the past.

For example, one CEO got to the top spot primarily because she was very focused on bottom-line results and was more efficient than her colleagues. When she was brought in to turn around a company, she dove into the numbers and immediately made some key changes, without spending a lot of time building trust with her team. I coached her on being more approachable and even "wasting" time, coming early to lunch meetings to chat with the team, or going out with the engineers for a beer after work. Although she certainly had the ability to make these changes, she was concerned that the impact might be too big—she would be sacrificing time that she could spend with clients, analyzing results, or designing products. It was hard to get her to make the change.

Also, senior people are more carefully watched, and they worry that if they make a mistake with a new approach, they will be seen as a failure or a fraud.

One young founder of a successful company had a hard time stepping out of the role of chief product officer and salesman because he worried that the company wouldn't succeed if he weren't putting out the fires in all areas. What he really needed to do, though, was to step back and let his functional leads fumble a bit and grow into their roles. He worried that by stepping back, he might look weak, or even unimportant to the company's future success—and yet it was only by stepping back that he could give himself the latitude to think about the company's next strategic moves.

What separates the truly great from the merely successful is often willingness to try something new or take a risk. This is especially true of senior executives, who may grow more risk-averse as they become established in leadership roles.

What are the critical assets and strengths of an outstanding coach?

A great coach is someone who is experienced with the processes you are developing, a good listener, responsive, and passionate, and someone with whom you have a good connection.

- *Experience.* The best coaches have done what they are trying to coach. As Alan says, they're like the ski instructor going down the mountain ahead of you—you know they know what they are talking about because they are doing it!

- *Listening skills.* Most good coaches are good listeners. They hear your particular issue and respond to it. They generally are brief, articulate, and consistent in their feedback, and above all, they are direct. When you are working with a coach, you want someone

who will tell you when you are doing something
wrong and when you are doing something right.

- *Responsiveness.* Coaches are responsive and available.
  You may need your coach to prep for the game, while
  you are playing, and after, so you want someone who
  can be on the sidelines—just a call or e-mail away.
- *Passion.* Good coaches are passionate about being
  coaches and are motivated by seeing their clients
  improve their condition as a result of the coaching.
  When you ask someone why he or she coaches,
  usually the person says something like, "Because I
  love it," or, "Because I can, and it makes such a
  difference."
- *Connection.* You are likely to have an honest and
  sometimes confrontational relationship with your
  coach, so it needs to be someone you feel you can
  trust and respect. I would suggest interviewing a few
  different coaches to assess fit, paying as much
  attention to the way you feel about working with the
  person as you do to the answers themselves. You want
  your coach to be someone whom you will want to
  call, confide in, and trust.

While I make my living advising other people, I still use a
coach (Alan is my primary mentor and has been for the past several years) for myself, to help me stay focused on my goals and
recognize when I'm being less effective than I could be.

INTERVIEW 9

Libby Wagner
Libby Wagner & Associates
Seattle, Washington

Why are some people "uncoachable"?
There are three main reasons that someone may be uncoachable: an unwillingness to be open to making changes in behavior, a diminished ability to reflect or self-assess, or a strong desire to remain in "victim mode," blaming others. Any or all of these make coaching nearly impossible, or at least incredibly challenging.

For example, an unwillingness to be open to changing behavior will create the same results this person is getting currently, so why waste his or your time? Growth involves taking some risk, which means that the person will have to make some behavioral changes, whether it's communication, decision making, or delegating, depending upon the coaching goals. The second uncoachable trait—the demonstrated inability to reflect or self-assess—may give you some indication of either a significant blind spot or some cognitive and/or personality traits that inhibit development. Again, because learning and growth involve self-assessment—"Well, that didn't go very well; how can I change it?" or, "That worked! I should do that again"— the coaching client must have some capacity for reflection in order to demonstrate progress or growth toward the intended outcomes or goals. Finally, if someone refuses to emerge from victim thinking, you can pretty much count on your coaching sessions veering off into the person's complaining, moaning, and groaning about how she is underappreciated, devalued, and misunderstood. This is not to say that organizational dysfunction or strained relationships may not indeed be inhibiting someone's growth or effectiveness, but everyone has the ability to choose how to respond to what's going on and make empowered choices, even if the choice is radical.

The good news is that it's fairly easy to assess whether someone is coachable or not within the first meeting or call. I typically ask some provocative questions that will allow me to ascertain if we are a good coaching fit together. These questions might include:

1. How will our working together make a difference in your leadership capabilities?
2. What do you see as three current obstacles to your increasing success as a leader?
3. How do you like to receive feedback? And, share a time when you received "good" feedback that caused you to make some changes in your behavior or practices.

The answers to these questions will give me some idea of the coaching client's willingness to change, self-assess, and take ownership.

Additionally, I will note that I have met very few uncoachable potential clients. Even those whose organizations or senior leadership have seen a need for coaching (developmental or remedial) will most likely see it as a way to improve, gain professional development, or get relief. Most of the time, resistance to coaching comes from fear—fear of failure, fear of losing face, or fear of not living up to one's own standards or expectations. Most people are coachable!

What are the keys in coaching entrepreneurs and business owners?

Coaching entrepreneurs and owners, especially those of small companies, is very similar in that they are often besieged by habits that create an imbalance between strategic behaviors and tactical behaviors. And, since they are entrepreneurial by nature (independent, good work ethic, creative, innovative, lack of attention to detail), coaching them often involves helping them put into place systems or practices to increase their discipline. Here are four keys to effective coaching of entrepreneurs and owners:

1. *Recognize that any decisions that they make will be filtered through a very personal lens.* This may seem obvious, but self-reliant individuals who set out on a quest to create their own independent, self-driven lives have their own personal mission up front and center for any decision they make, whether it's how to invest their money, time, development dollars, or something else. Initially, they may be reluctant to invest in coaching for themselves because it seems like a luxury expense rather than a necessary means to an end— their growth and development. They will always, whether it's out loud or subconsciously, be wondering, "What's in it for me?" and, "How will this further my most immediate goals?" You can help coach and guide them by demonstrating how investing in themselves will be one of the single best long-term leveraging activities for success in business and in life. They often seek coaching to get closer to that ever-elusive notion of "work/life balance."

2. *They often need help in managing and mastering their time, since they often believe that doing everything themselves will save them time and money.* Almost all entrepreneurs and owners start out being the cook, baker, and chief bottle washer. As they grow, they continue these behaviors, either being in the midst of

everything they're trying to get their employees to do, or wasting time trying to create their own Web sites and balance their books. They move farther and farther away from setting aside time for strategic thinking and innovation by dealing with operational issues and fighting fires. Depending on the scenario, sometimes your coaching can help them prioritize and make decisions about how to grow their business, increase their happiness, and improve their life balance by figuring out what not to do. Their energies can be scattered and fragmented because they are trying to do so much themselves, and you can help them create focus and accountabilities via your coaching goals and follow-up. Help them implement practices that encourage systems, efficiencies, and ease of execution.

3. *They often struggle with implementation and execution of their strategy.* This is certainly related to point 2, since the primary reason that they're not spending enough (or any!) time thinking strategically, carving out time for creative dreaming, or cultivating relationships that support those activities is that they are dealing with their business. Or, they are frittering away time (since they're often alone, some can really fritter . . .) on activities that are task-oriented or not even in alignment with their overall strategic vision. Mostly, this has to do with self-confidence and self-esteem, along with discipline. When we are certain of our vision, and we are self-confident in that knowledge, we know what to say yes to and what to refuse. When we are solid in this conviction, we behave purposefully and gain increased energy around the discipline we need if we are to succeed.

4. *Since entrepreneurs are often "lone wolves," or, if owners, they have no peers in proximity, they often do not have the give-and-take of peer relationships, and they may want to befriend you.* Good coaches have varying views on whether or not the coaching relationship is strictly business, or whether it's okay to develop friendships with your clients. I have mixed feelings myself, but one thing that I do is set clear boundaries, especially about access to me, and I try to stick to my promises to myself. For example, entrepreneurs and small business owners prefer to meet face-to-face rather than having coaching calls. I try to manage this, since often a face-to-face meeting does not necessarily create more value for the client or help me maintain my workload goals. Because of the nature of my specific type of coaching—leadership, communication, team development, conflict resolution, influencing—the skills spill over into personal lives, and coaching clients often ask me about navigating their personal relationships. I do not refuse to answer questions, but I also make sure that I know my boundaries concerning what is coaching—future-focused and developmental—and what is counseling—something that I'm not prepared or inclined to do. I always draw this line and share that I can make recommendations or referrals, if that would be helpful. Sharing personal information or disclosing your own stories creates relationship and trust, and you are in a relationship with your coaching client, but it's important to maintain the focus on the client. This is more art than science, for sure, but I am always careful about sharing personal stories or anecdotes that don't have a direct correlation or helpful angle to the work or work/life-balance-related issues we are working on.

INTERVIEW 10

Andrew Sobel
Andrew Sobel Advisors, Inc.
Santa Fe, New Mexico

What are the critical assets and strengths of an outstanding coach?

I've interviewed a number of great coaches, and they all have very different styles and approaches to coaching. Some are blunt and assertive, while others, equally successful, are more soft-spoken in their approach. Some have very specific coaching methodologies that they adhere to religiously, while others are more adaptable. There are, however, five core attributes that I think nearly all great coaches bring to their clients. These are qualities that will set you apart from the average professional. They are empathy, big-picture thinking, knowledge depth and breadth—being a "deep generalist," self-awareness, and selfless independence. Let's briefly look at each one.

Empathy is the ability to perceive and feel someone else's feelings. In coaching, I think about empathy even more broadly. To be able to diagnose and prescribe for a client, you have to tune into that client's thoughts and context as well as his or her feelings. To do this well, you must be a good listener—you have to have the patience to carefully explore a client's situation and the issues he or she faces by asking thoughtful questions and listening closely to the answers. If you don't empathize well, the other person will not open up to you, and your advice will be based on an incomplete understanding of the problem.

Big-picture thinking, or the ability to synthesize information, is another hallmark of successful coaches. When you analyze a problem, you break it down into pieces—you tear it apart. When you synthesize, however, you bring all the pieces back together and see the patterns and the trends. I had a coaching client who had suffered a series of mishaps at work. We could have simply analyzed each one, and come up with the best possible advice for dealing with each awkward situation. Instead, I looked at what these incidents had in common, and then tied them back to a developmental issue that my client had not really confronted. As a result, these incidents dried up, which would not have happened if I had applied purely analytical thinking. Good coaches, in short, pull their clients out of the weeds.

One of the principal ways to improve your powers of synthesis is to become what I call a *deep generalist*. A deep generalist has a core specialty (or specialties) but also a breadth of knowledge around that expertise—he is a "T-shaped" professional. A really good coach will complement her coaching skills with, potentially, industry knowledge, process or functional knowledge, and general business acumen. This breadth enables you to make the knowledge connections that are the hallmark of big-picture thinkers, and it sets you apart from the competition.

A fourth essential attribute for coaches is *self-awareness*. Given the intimate, one-on-one nature of coaching, you have to have a handle on your own biases, hot buttons, insecurities, and other foibles—otherwise you risk having an emotional or intellectually flawed response to something that your client says or does. If a client misses an appointment, chronically interrupts you, or is appeasing a totalitarian boss at work (who reminds you of someone you used to work for who made you miserable), do you have a level of self-awareness and self-understanding that enables you to always respond in a businesslike, unemotional way?

Finally, great coaches have independence—or, better yet, *selfless independence*. They are devoted to their clients and to helping them improve, but at the same time they offer complete objectivity and independence. A client needs to know that his coach will always put the client's interests first, and yet at the same time will always tell it to the client the way the coach sees it, even if the truth hurts.

There are certainly other skills and strengths that help you to be a good coach—intelligence, hard work, communications skills, and so on—but these are necessary but not sufficient if you wish to truly stand apart from the crowd. The five attributes mentioned here can, on the other hand, tip you over the edge toward greatness.

What is your opinion of coaching "universities" and certifications?

Clients hire coaches based on their experience and the value they can deliver. Coaching certifications and accreditations may be useful to you as a professional, but they are not going to magically convert you into a masterful executive coach or convince a client to choose you over others. There are three main reasons why this is true.

First, coaching is not a profession in the way that accounting, law, and medicine are. In a profession, there is a universally accepted qualification, such as the CPA for accountants and the MD for doctors. These are accepted because there is a defined body of knowledge that all certified practitioners must master, with no exceptions. Professions also have recognized boards or associations that have the power to sanction their members for professional misconduct. Usually, these qualifications are also very difficult and time-consuming to earn—think about four years to complete medical school, for example. Coaching—like management consulting—is really an avocation, a career field.

There is no single standard degree—many organizations offer "coaching" credentialing—and the requirements pale in comparison to a real professional certification. Clients are smart: if you have an MBA, an MSW, or a Ph.D., they understand that you had to put in several or more years of hard work to earn that degree; they also know that a coaching certification could have been obtained in a matter of weeks.

A second reason why coaching certifications may be personally useful but not meaningful in the marketplace has to do with the vast diversity of the coaching practice. Some coaches, for example, have backgrounds in psychology and focus on behavioral issues and helping executives stop dysfunctional behavior that is holding back their careers. Others could be termed "performance coaches" who have subject matter and industry expertise, along with a knack for helping their clients set goals and achieve them. Yet others specialize in areas such as career coaching or executive presence and communications. No single coaching certification program can possibly address the diversity of coaching practice, just as even a two-year MBA degree does not "certify" that graduates have equally mastered human resources management, finance, and operations.

Finally, a number of studies have shown that when choosing a coach, clients look first at experience. They are asking, "Do you have the requisite experience to tackle this particular coaching assignment?" Because of my background and reputation, for example, I am often hired to work with executives on business development and client relationship issues; in contrast, I would not be seen as the right coach for an executive with self-destructive behavioral issues. When marketing yourself to clients, focus on the areas that they will be concerned about. They will be asking:

1. Do you have the combination of management experience, functional or industry expertise, and

coaching experience that we need for this assignment?

2. Do you have a track record of success, as evidenced by word-of-mouth referrals and strong references from past clients?

3. Do you have other degrees or accreditations that lend weight to your expertise—for example, a graduate degree in a relevant field (business, psychology, or some other area)?

A coaching degree or certification may be a small "plus" in the column of assets that you offer, and it may be helpful to you personally in terms of skill development and networking. For your clients, however, it will pale in comparison to these other major factors as a reason to hire you.

INTERVIEW 11

Dan Weedin
Toro Consulting, Inc.
Poulsbo, Washington

What is the role or advantage of using technology in coaching?
Executive and business coaches who don't take full advantage of technology are spending too much of their own time and not helping their clients as well as they could. Not being technologically savvy is a bad excuse. The advantages are too great for the coach and the client.

The advantages of using technology in coaching are threefold:

1. *The ability of the coach to respond quickly to a question or concern is elevated.* For instance, text messaging provides almost instantaneous access. A person who is being coached may require an immediate answer because she is going into an important meeting or preparing to walk on stage to speak. The use of text messaging can give the coach the means to provide a pithy, yet valuable response just in time to aid the client.

   I recently had a client text me a question before going into a meeting with a major prospect. He prefers to text because sometimes his phone reception is dicey. I was able to quickly respond to his question, and he made the sale.

2. *Technology bridges distance and relationship.* With the evolution of platforms like Skype™ and Go to Meeting®, coaches and clients can meet anywhere, any time, and face to face. We are an increasingly visual society, and the importance of carrying on even a short meeting face to face improves both access and relationship.

   One of my clients across the state had a business issue related to risk management. I was able to show my process visuals and explain the concept via a quickly convened Go to Meeting meeting. His needs were more effectively and efficiently met, and I never had to leave my office. The total time invested was 15 minutes.

3. *Coaching becomes more attractive to busy people.* Many consultants and industry experts who would make terrific coaches may have avoided coaching because of a perceived increase in labor intensity. Ever-

advancing technology provides a way to respond to client requests more efficiently and quickly, thus making coaching more attractive as an additional revenue-generating part of their practice. The results of this include improving the careers of many clients who can gain immeasurable aid from these experts.

The bottom line is that technology improves clients by getting them the answers they need, when they need them, and in a format they want. It improves coaches by reducing labor intensity and travel time. As technology advances, it will undoubtedly mean increased opportunities for coaches to provide better value to more clients.

What are the critical assets and strengths of an outstanding coach?

Every truly remarkable coach, whether in business or in athletics, has certain critical assets and strengths as common denominators. They may all express them a little differently based on their own unique personality, but they are certainly there. Here are my top nine qualities:

1. *Excellent listener.* Coaches can't get caught up in their own noise. They must be able to proactively listen to clients without predetermining their responses. Being a good listener takes patience, humility, and self-control. The coaches who truly can master this quality will do more for their clients and their own business.

2. *Ability to frame situations.* Clients call coaches when they are confused or overwhelmed. Good coaches must be able to take a chaotic situation (at least in the mind of the client) and frame it in an easy-to-swallow

overview. In my experience, my mentors have been able to do this and have helped me be able to take control of what seemed to be a difficult issue and break it down to its simplest form. Once there, it is much easier to deal with.

3. *Doesn't just provide answers.* The famous axiom about teaching a man to fish rather than giving him a fish applies here. Too may times, clients want the solution immediately. Good coaches help steer them in the right direction so that they can learn the process themselves.

4. *Excellent communicator.* Being clear, concise, and pithy are wonderful assets for a good coach. The better a coach can communicate the message to his or her clients, the quicker those clients are improved.

5. *Has been there and done that.* You don't find great athletic coaches who have never played the sport or been privy to masters before them. The same is true in business coaching. A strength for any coach is his or her experience. The client must count on the coach as having been where the client wants to go, or else the client is simply wasting time.

6. *Accessible.* Outstanding coaches must be accessible. If a client can't rely on his or her coach being there when the client needs him or her most, it will result in a bad relationship. Determining base levels of communication and access are critical to gaining full trust and results.

7. *Honest.* It does the client no good if the coach isn't honest in his or her assessments and advice. Every outstanding coach has their unique personality to deliver that honesty; however, the truly great ones get that message quickly and powerfully to their clients.

8. *Empathetic.* An outstanding coach feels for his or her clients. When a coach can be humble enough to feel empathy, this will engender a strong relationship and more open communications.

9. *Continues to grow.* You don't want a coach who thinks he or she has learned everything that he or she needs to know. Clients need coaches who will continually challenge themselves to learn, develop, and grow. Not only is this superb role modeling, but also it ensures that the coach will always be at the top of his or her game, which is what a client needs.

What are the keys in coaching entrepreneurs and business owners?

Everyone needs a coach. Often, entrepreneurs and business owners don't seek one out because they don't know that the concept exists for them, they don't think they need any help, or they are too proud to admit that they do need help. If this is your market, or you want it to be, you must keep three key factors in mind when you coach entrepreneurs and owners.

1. *Many entrepreneurs and small business owners aren't familiar with the coaching format.* They are used to "running the show" themselves. Sometimes being "coachable" is a challenge. Remind them that the reason they hired you was to help them move forward on their issues and that if they could do it themselves, you wouldn't be needed. They can choose to ignore you, but that defeats the purpose of coaching, and they will probably get the same results they always got.

2. *Some entrepreneurs will be concerned about your lack of industry knowledge of their field.* This is actually a benefit. Not having been corrupted by the industry thinking helps you help them.

I was talking with a restaurant owner about helping her enhance her brand and marketing strategy. She said, "Dan, it sounds great, but I'm concerned that you don't have any experience in the restaurant business." My response was, "You're right, I don't. However, I have a lot of experience eating at restaurants. I know what works in getting me in their door." After about three seconds of stunned silence, she hired me on the spot. Your coaching prospects must understand that your unbiased viewpoint is just what they need.

3. *You must be considered a peer.* If you are viewed as a commodity, the respect and credibility will not be there. In fact, you probably wouldn't have been hired in this case. It's important to keep this level of equality throughout your coaching through your language, your pushback, your challenging, and your time management.

This was one of the most difficult things for me to learn in developing my practice. I came from an insurance sales environment where the prospect was "always right," even though he or she very often wasn't. When you consider yourself in constant competition, you avoid doing anything to make waves. In hindsight, that may be the very thing that differentiates you from the competition. When I went into my consulting practice, this was a slow hurdle to leap over, but eventually, with a paradigm shift, I was able to get there. That same level of confidence is needed in coaching because entrepreneurs don't want you to be a "yes-man or -woman." They already have enough of those in their organization.

INDEX

and dealing with true buyers,
169–173
and determining the budget
range, 257–258
licensing, 222
and price vs. value, 174–178
and retainers, 57–58, 162–165
value-based, 157–161
Financial strategists, 9
Focus groups, 60
Follow-up, 125–126
Follow-up questions, 250
"Forced choice" tests, 116
Formal rehearsals, 111
Fourth sale first, thinking of the,
139, 143
Frame of reference, keeping a
wide, 180–181
Fripp, Patricia, 192, 216

Games, 61, 108
Gardner, John, 192
Gatekeepers, 50
Getting Started in Consulting
(Weiss), 211
Girl Scouts, 151
Gitomer, Jeff, 132, 192
Gladwell, Malcolm, 192
Goals, buyer's, 30
Godin, Seth, 132, 191
Goldsmith, Marshall, 132, 181,
191, 195, 227
Google Alerts, 198
Google Search, 217
Gossip, avoiding, 89
Government clients, 151
Growth, "S curve" for, 181–182

Halsey, William F., 244
Handouts, 218
Havlicek, John, 17*n*3
Help, asking for, 29
Hewlett-Packard, 14, 96, 123*n*2
Hierarchy of needs, 242–243

Hill, Napoleon, 243
Homework, doing your, 30
Honesty, 306
Hour, charging by the, 56,
157–158
House publications (house organs),
142
*How to Write a Proposal That's
Accepted Every Time* (Alan
Weiss), 50*n*1
Human Resources (HR), 41
Humor, sense of, 275

Identifying a need, 11
Impact, demonstrating, 38
Implicit knowledge, 120
Improvable points, focusing on, 37
Improve, desire to, 11–12
In-basket exercises, 61
Independent experts, 202
Innovation:
focusing on, 197
providing, 207
Instantiation, 184
Instrumented techniques,
103–107, 115–119
Instruments, assessment, 61
Integrity, 4
Intellectual property, 48, 193,
214–218, 221
Intellectual respect, 32
Interpersonal techniques, 91–95
assessment, 92
observation and feedback,
91–92
rehearsals and role-plays,
92–93
serendipity, 94–95
360-degree assessments,
93–94
Interviews:
as methodology, 60, 61
print, 144
radio, 147

ABOUT THE AUTHOR

ALAN WEISS is one of those rare people who can say that he is a consultant, speaker, and author and mean it. His consulting firm, Summit Consulting Group, Inc., has attracted clients such as Merck, Hewlett-Packard, GE, Mercedes-Benz, State Street Corporation, Times Mirror Group, the Federal Reserve, the New York Times Corporation, and more than 500 other leading organizations. He has served on the boards of directors of the Trinity Repertory Company, a Tony Award–winning New England regional theater, Festival Ballet, and has chaired the Newport International Film Festival.

His speaking typically includes 30 keynotes a year at major conferences, and he has been a visiting faculty member at Case Western Reserve University, Boston College, Tufts, St. John's, the University of Illinois, the Institute of Management Studies, and the University of Georgia Graduate School of Business. He has held an appointment as adjunct professor in the Graduate School of Business at the University of Rhode Island, where he taught courses on advanced management and consulting skills. He holds the record for selling out the highest-priced workshop (on entrepreneurialism) in the 21-year history of New York City's Learning Annex. His Ph.D. is in psychology, and he is a member of the American Psychological Society, the American Counseling Association, Division 13 of the American Psychological Association, and the Society for Personality and Social Psychology. He has served on the board of governors of Harvard University's Center for Mental Health and the Media.

He has keynoted for the American Psychological Association on two occasions.

Alan has been inducted into the Professional Speaking Hall of Fame and concurrently received the National Speakers Association Council of Peers Award of Excellence, representing the top 1 percent of professional speakers in the world. He has been named a Fellow of the Institute of Management Consultants (FCMC), one of only two people in history holding both those designations.

His prolific publishing includes more than 500 articles and 40 books, including his bestseller, *Million Dollar Consulting* (from McGraw-Hill). His books have been on the curricula at Villanova, Temple University, and the Wharton School of Business, and have been translated into German, Italian, Arabic, Spanish, Russian, Korean, and Chinese.

He is interviewed and quoted frequently in the media. His career has taken him to 57 countries and 49 states. (He is afraid to go to North Dakota.) *Success* magazine has cited him in an editorial devoted to his work as "a worldwide expert in executive education." The *New York Post* calls him "one of the most highly regarded independent consultants in America." He is the winner of the prestigious Axiem Award for Excellence in Audio Presentation.

In 2006 he was presented with the Lifetime Achievement Award of the American Press Institute, the first ever for a non-journalist, and one of only seven awarded in the 60+-year history of the association.

He has coached the Miss Rhode Island/Miss America candidates in interviewing skills. He once appeared on the popular American TV game show *Jeopardy*, where he lost badly in the first round to a dancing waiter from Iowa.

Alan Weiss, Ph.D.

President

Summit Consulting Group, Inc.

Box 1009

East Greenwich, RI 02818

Phone: 401/884-2778   Fax: 401/884-5068

Alan@summitconsulting.com

http://www.summitconsulting.com

Visit Our Web Site for

- A subscription to our free, monthly electronic newsletter: *Balancing Act: Blending Life, Work, and Relationships*
- Inclusion on our notification list for new products, workshops, and services
- Access to over 100 free, indexed articles
- Access to a variety of other resources for self-development and professional growth